Divine Light

Yoga Systems with Their Secret Techniques

S.K. Das

New Age Books

ISBN: 978-81-7822-097-0

Reprint: Delhi, 2008
Second Revised Edition: Delhi, 2002

Published by
NEW AGE BOOKS
A-44 Naraina Phase-I
New Delhi-110 028 (INDIA)
Email: nab@vsnl.in
Website: www.newagebooksindia.com

Printed in India
at Shri Jainendra Press
A-45 Naraina Phase-I, New Delhi-110 028

PUBLISHER'S NOTE

The book by Shri Shrikrishna Das was first published in 1953 and had run two more editions during his lifetime before, in view of its great popularity and public utility, we agreed to reissue it on the wise advice of Shri Surendra Anand in a form edited by Dr. G.P. Bhatt. We acknowledge our heart-felt gratefulness individually to all these scholars for enabling us to re-publish their pious and nice small book.

CONTENTS

PART II: INVOCATIONS AND MISCELLANEOUS

FOREWORD

Wonder of wonders it is that even human beings, endowed with a superior intelligence by Benign Creator, are not ashamed of leading an aimless life, a life without an ideal, a life without any purpose at all! Beloved Image of God! Did the Lord marvel at you, the crowning glory of Creation only because you could be more bestial than beasts themselves, you could eat and drink with more avidity and less sense than the animals, you could indulge the senses more intelligently and therefore, more thoroughly than animals, that you could destroy yourselves and others in the twinkling of an eye with your superior intelligence, powerful intellect and scientific knowledge !

No! The Lord marvelled at His own creation of man because in Man had creation attained perfection, in man had been perfected the consciousness that had remained latent, dormant and undeveloped in other forms of creation, in man had been placed the capacity to know the Creator, become one with Him. To man had been given the capacity to know "I and my Father are one." Upon man had been bestowed the glorious privilege of realising that consciousness that linked him with his creator, the consciousness in which he and the Supreme Being are one.

Just as a father rejoices at the birth of a son who would soon take his place, who would identify his interests with the father's and virtually become one with him, even so God rejoiced at the evolving life principle when it entered man who would rejoin Him, love Him and become one with Him in consciousness. That is the purpose with which man is born here. That is the glorious ideal which every man should hold before himself.

But, what do we find today? It is a story of the woodcutter whom a saint met in his wanderings. The saint asked the woodcutter, "Friend, why do you cut wood?" "To feed my belly, Sir." "Why do you feed the belly?" "To cut wood, Maharaj." Is there any sense in such a life? You laugh ! But, is it not true that almost everyone lives in this fashion today?

Face is the index of mind; your book-shelf is the index of your culture. Tell me what books you love most; I will tell you what your level of intelligence is. What sorts of books adorn the book-shelves of our modern, fashionable, educated and cultured brethren? Sensational novels, detective stories, nerve titillating romantic dramas and crime books. That is the index of your "superior intelligence"! A buffalo would go on chewing hay at the bidding of its natural hunger! But intelligent man cares not for Nature's demand for food, for he can create it by condiments. He can create sense-pleasure by reading filthy stories, and satisfy the craving by licentious indulgence. That is the mark of your "superior intelligence" which makes even God rejoice!

While the vulgar sensualist craves for excitement, the greedy bania sees his opportunity in it; and he produces endless stream of soul-killing stuff, "hot-cakes" and "best-sellers". Between them they ruin the younger generation. The vicious circle is now complete.

Svadhyaya or study of books is a part of yoga. Why have our ancients given to it a place of honour in their scheme of Yoga-Sadhana? They knew that it ennobled the spirit of man, it helped the aspirant's mind to dwell for ever in the sublime region of spiritual glory, and more than anything else, it held before man's mind divine idea, the great goal, and inspired man to reach it. A scripture is your Guru-in-book-form.

When will our educationists realise this? When will our publishers realise this? They must cut the Gordian knot. They must bravely come forward and rescue our culture from the cruel grip of the sensualist. They must raise literature once again to the lofty heights of our inspirer of man to glorious endeavours, to attain the goal of life on earth, the purpose of human birth—realisation of God. Then would we have fulfilled the purpose for which God created us.

I, therefore, welcome this inestimable addition to the spiritual literature of the country. Wisely, Shri S.K. Das has incorporated into this volume his essays on a variety of spiritual matters, including the life of a glorious Maharshi Shri Ramana. Thus, he has brought within the cover of one handy book, theoretical knowledge as well as wholesome practical advice, supplemented by the actual life-story of an exemplar. The book is, therefore, highly inspiring.

Shri S.K. Das is an able journalist with a facile pen which he has always used for the uplift of man for the elevation of his consciousness. He has been a regular contributor during his student career to several journals, and has been an ardent student of Vedanta. These inspiring essays have appeared in several magazines and have created wide appreciation.

I wish every student and every literate man and woman of this country, and of the whole world at large, to take advantage of this labour of love on the part of Shri S.K. Das, study these essays with faith and devotion and be inspired by them.

May God bless Shri Das with health, long life, peace, prosperity and Atma-Jnana! May His blessing be showered upon all!

SWAMI SIVANANDA
Founder President
Divine Life Society

Rishikesh
14th July, 1952

PREFACE

Look to this day,
For this is life,
The very life of life,
For yesterday is already a dream,
And tomorrow is only a vision,
But today well-lived,
Makes every yesterday a dream
And every tomorrow a vision of hope.

—*Oscar Wilde*

Art is long and life is short. If we spend life after life for the attainment of complete knowledge of a dust particle, it may prove a futile effort, as knowledge will go on unfolding itself ad infinitum. The more we claim to know, the more we discover our ignorance and limitation. The recent discoveries about atom, and its vast and wonderful powers and potentialities, are well-known.

India is famous for its spiritual advancement. Our ancient seers and sages have devoted themselves wholly in finding the Truth. From the time immemorial, they have been making experiments with the Self. There is so much spiritual literature in Hinduism (viz. Vedas, Upanishads, Puranas, Smritis, two great epics, Ramayana and Mahabharata, Bhagavad Gita, Yoga Shastras, Tantras and so forth) that one cannot study them all even if one spends life after life for this purpose.

While we acknowledge the vastness of knowledge and our inability and limitation to its attainment, we feel that in actual practice, during the course of our lives, we can utilise only an insignificant fraction of it, just as we can make use of seconds from the eternal cycle of time, at a time.

Attainment of knowledge is not sufficient unless it is made use of. Knowledge which cannot be brought into practice is not worth having or giving. Knowledge without action is like a canal without water, a flower without fragrance. It is well said that truths of life can be counted on finger tips. The secret of success lies in using these truths and moulding them into our lives. Knowledge is like a field and action is the sowing of seeds. So the conclusion is that while knowledge is limitless and transcends the flight of human thought, we should pick up the knowledge pertaining to our immediate needs and duties in life according to our status and position and bring that knowledge into practice, to derive full benefit. There are many scholars, philosophers and intellectual giants, but there are few, who really do what they know and teach. The world follows the men of action and not the preachers. An example of the late Mahatma Gandhi can be aptly quoted, as it is very familiar to us. The secret of his greatness and influence was his ability and capacity to translate his precepts into actions before preaching to others. Unless he did and could do a thing himself, he would not preach to others. In Mahabharata, we find an interesting anecdote. Yudhishthira, the eldest brother of Pandavas, was once asked by his Guru (teacher) to memorise a lesson from a book, the first passage of which was something like this: 'Control anger as it destroys clear understanding'. Yudhishthira was asked to recite his lesson, but he said that he could only learn the first passage thereof. Next day the same reply was given. The Guru got annoyed and gave him a severe beating. Yudhishthira was calm and quiet. At last the Guru realised that he himself was wrong and that Yudhishthira was right in actually learning what he was taught, as he did not get angry and kept calm. Numerous other examples can be quoted. We derive benefit to the extent we make use of any object. Knowledge not in use is like money stored in chests and vaults of a strong room or a treasure hidden in the gold mine. Persons acting on principles have attained the highest goal, while persons full of book-lore have miserably failed in life. Devotees who had little knowledge of scriptures attained to Godhead simply by selfless devotion. It is the actual action that gives life to the ideas and thoughts. Castles in the air should be followed by castles on the earth, or it will otherwise be vain and wishful thinking. World requires practical men and women. In the words of Shri J. Krishnamurti, "this is total integration of thought and action without which life is unreal and meaningless."

We should, therefore, act on what we know to be good and useful for ourselves and others.

Knowledge of the self is the key to all knowledge. It is superior to any other kind of knowledge. It is that by knowing which everything is known. "Seek ye the kingdom of God and everything shall be added unto thee." Science of Eternal (Brahma Vidya) is the basis of all knowledge. **(ब्रह्मविद्या सर्वविद्या)**

This is the source of all sciences, the means of performing all actions and the support of all duties. As this leads to find beatitude of life, so it is regarded as chief among all kinds of knowledge. We can attain the knowledge of self by adopting a right attitude in life and keeping conformity in our thoughts and actions. Skill in action is Yoga and to perform one's duties selflessly for the sake of duty is the highest Yajna. Yoga is relating oneself (yoking) to the Supreme Power that rules the Universe. It means the discipline by which the central being within us remains balanced under all conditions, through understanding. This is the crux of the teachings of Gita, which is the most beautiful and eternal Song of philosophy known to human race with its universal message.* Here is the Golden Path by following which a man in the world can reach the highest realms of happiness and glory while living and moving in the world and attending to all his duties. It teaches us the art of living, the art of union with Supreme Soul and the secret of eternal happiness.

The following pages contain some deep-felt thoughts of the writer. These were written under inspiration at exalted moments.

The purpose of bringing out this book is to create an interest and inspiration towards divinity and to share with my readers many secret and sacred Sadhanas which I have picked up during my lifetime from study and by sitting at the holy feet of saints and seers, like Bhagavan Ramana Maharshi, His Holiness Swami Sivananda Saraswati, Maharshi Mahesh Yogi, Her Holiness Vimala Thakar, Bhakti Vedanta Swami Prabhu Pada, Acharya Amritavagbhava, Swami Lakshmana Joo, Sri Gopikrishana, Sri Guruji of Varasani, and many others.

An attempt has also been made to present the thoughts from rational point of view in order to make them amenable to sense of logic. The readers will, I believe, find these pages interesting, useful and of practical utility in their life, irrespective of their faith, caste and creed. They are also requested to look to the message rather than to the humble messanger!

May the Divine Light, the Light of lights, the all-filling Light, the eye-catching Light, the heart-touching Light, shine and manifest within us all!

S. K. DAS

---

* "The most beautiful, perhaps the only true philosophical song existing in any known tongue." — Wilhelm von Humboldt

PRAYER

स तन्मयो ह्यमृत ईशसंस्थो ज्ञः सर्वगो
भुवनस्यास्य गोप्ता।
य ईशे अस्य जगतो नित्यमेव
नान्यो हेतुर्विद्यत ईशनाय॥

Svetasvatara Upanishad

He is the Universal Soul and Immortal; His is the Rulership; He is the Omniscient, the All-prevading, the Protector of the Universe, the Eternal Ruler. None else is there so competent to govern the world eternally.

यो ब्रह्माणं विदधाति पूर्वं
यो वै वेदांश्च प्रहिणोति तस्मै।
तं ह देवमात्मबुद्धिप्रकाशं
मुमुक्षुर्वै शरणमहं प्रपद्ये।

Svetasvatara Upanishad

He Who at the beginning of creation projected Universal Consciousness (Brahma) and Who delivered the Vedas unto him — seeking liberation, I go for refuge unto that Effulgent One, Whose Divine Light turns the understanding towards Atman.

प्रभो शम्भो! दीनं विहितशरणं त्वच्चरणयो-
र्भवारण्यादस्माद्विषमविषयाशीविषवृतात्।
समुद्धृत्य श्रद्धाविधुरमपि बद्धादरकरं
दयादृष्ट्या पश्यन्निजतनयमात्मीकुरु शिव॥

Acharya Sri Amritavagbhava

O, Thou Almighty, All-merciful, All-benevolent God ! Thou Embodiment of Grace and Love! Pray save me from the transient objects of senses, which are like snakes in the forest of the world. Lead me to

Thy Glorious Self as Thy Own, though I lack devotion, yet I have taken refuge in Thee, being disappointed on all sides. Pray accept my humble self-surrender*!

सुषारथिरश्वानिव यन् मनुष्यान्
नेनीयतेऽभीशुभिर्वाजिन इन
हृत्प्रतिष्टं यदजिरं जविष्ठं
तन्मे मनः शिवसंकल्पमस्तु ॥

Yajurveda

As a good rider controls the over-active horses with the help of the rein, so the Mind, ever youthful and active which dwells in the brain, controls the men. May that Mind of mine, be filled with ennobling and elevating thoughts!

असतो मा सद्गमय
तमसो मा ज्योतिर्गमय।
मृत्योर्मा अमृतं गमय।

From unreal lead me to the Real,
From darkness lead me to Light
From death, lead me to Immortality!

GAYATRI MANTRA

ओम् भूर्भुवः स्वः तत्सवितुर्वरेण्यं भर्गो देवस्य धीमहि धियो यो नः प्रचोदयात् ॥

Rigveda III.62.10

Let us meditate on Isvara** (Savitr) and His glory (devasya) who has created the Universe, Who is fit to be worshipped (varenyam), Who is the remover of all sins and ignorance. May He enlighten our intellect!

HARI STOTRA

शांताकारं भुजंगशयनं पद्मनाभं सुरेशं
विश्वाधारं गगनसदृशं मेघवर्णं शुभाङ्गम्
लक्ष्मीकान्तं कमलनयनं योगिभिर्ध्यानगम्यं
वन्दे विष्णुं भवभयहरं सर्वलोकैकनाथम्॥

---

* This is a Siddha mantra composed and seen by Acharya Sri Amritavagbhava. It has been printed in lakhs with Hindi and English translations. Its recitation has yielded good results in all known cases.

** Primordial cause.

I bow to that Lord Vishnu, whose form is Peace,
Who lies on the bed of snake,
Who has lotus in the naval,
Who is lord of Gods,
Who is the support of the world,
Whose limbs are beautiful,
Who is the husband of Goddess Lakshmi,
Whose eyes are like Lotuses,
Who is attainable by yogins through meditation,
Who destroys the fear of samsara and
Who is one Lord of all the Creation.

MRITYUNJAYA MANTRA

ॐ त्र्यंबकं यजामहे सुगंधिं पुष्टिवर्द्धनम्।
उर्वारुकमिव बन्धनात्, मृत्योर्मुक्षीय मामृतात्॥

I bow to That three-eyed Lord Shiva, who is full of sweet fragrance, who nourishes the human beings (always). May He free me from the bondage of Samsara and death, just as a ripe fruit is naturally separated from the tree.

य एकोऽवर्णो बहुधा शक्तियोगाद्वर्णाननेकान् निहितार्थो दधाति।
वि चैति चान्ते विश्वमादौ स देवः स नो बुद्ध्या शुभया संयुनक्तु॥

The one without colour appears
by the manifold application of his power
with many colours of his hidden purpose.
May the Being of Splendor in whom the world dissolves
and from whom it rises.
Grant us a clear understanding.

Svetasvatara Upanishad

पूर्णमदः पूर्णमिदं पूर्णात्पूर्णमुदच्यते।
पूर्णस्य पूर्णमादाय पूर्णमेवावशिष्यते॥

The whole is beyond, whole is this (Creation)
From whole, the whole emanates
Of whole, the whole having taken
The whole alone is left over.

PART I

IMPORTANT YOGA SYSTEMS AND SECRET TECHNIQUES

1

THE AIM IN LIFE

"Whoever departs from this world without having realised his own inner world, to him life has been of no service; it remains unlived, like the unrecited Vedas or any other undone deed."

Brihadaranyaka Upanishad, 1.4.15.

Everyone will laugh at a traveller who is going on without knowing where he is going or where he has to go. Similarly, most of us continue our journey of life without knowing our goal and drift like a leaf in a running stream! Why we have come in this world and what is the real purpose of life, are the preliminary and important questions, which will give colour to our actions and thoughts and will lead us to the right or wrong direction.

If the purpose of human existence on earth is to eat, drink and be merry, there appears to be no difference between a man and an animal! Because in eating, drinking and sexual enjoyment both are nearly equal. Rather a man can indulge in them more lavishly than a beast, and can violate the limits and laws of nature. What is that which distinguishes man from beast, who proclaims his superiority over all the creatures of the earth? God has made man in his own image and bestowed upon him choicest virtues, superior intellect and intelligence, which make him the master of the world. He can tame ferocious lions, mighty elephants, whales and poisonous snakes, can overcome mountains, cross oceans, fly in the air and perform other miracles of his mastery over nature. He has walked on the surface of the moon. He is trying to reach other planets in the solar system. There is nothing in this world which he cannot do or accomplish within his sphere. He is superior to gods in certain respects. A great living yogi once told me that God has to obey the commands of human soul. Human soul is like a calf and God is like a cow. God will go after man to carry out his wishes, but all this is possible when man is really 'man'. This body is a miniature of this vast universe

(यथा ब्रह्माण्डे तथा पिण्डे). Human birth is difficult to get. This birth offers golden opportunity for sowing seeds for such *karmas* as can raise him to Godhood !

It appears, therefore, that there is some superior and sublime purpose of human life on earth, other than the enjoyment of sensual pleasures. Our aim in life should be consistent with that purpose. It should be other than eating and drinking, other than getting fame and fortune and other than enjoyment of sex or company of beautiful women. Drifting aimlessly will not lead us anywhere and there is a likelihood of our going astray from the path and losing ourselves in the wilderness of transitory pleasures.

The final and ultimate aim of human existence is the realization of Self. 'Know Thyself' and 'Thou art That' have to be realised practically. Man has to remove the sheath of ignorance and to discover his identity with the Universal Self, the infinite source of Existence, Knowledge and Bliss.

This means that man will have to break his limitations of small 'self' and to extend it to all creatures and the Universe. He will have to see the same Self everywhere and to love it as he loves himself and to live and work for the welfare of humanity. He loses the sense of duality. All the world will appear to him as his own image. His self is not confined to his body and family. It extends from his street and city to his country and then to the whole world. He will not work for small selfish ends or gain but for the sake of his duty towards his fellow-beings. Service of humanity is the service of God and is the highest form of worship. He may have any subsidiary or immediate aim in life but this ultimate motive of life will add grace, glory and significance to that and will crown his efforts with real success and happiness.

It is not necessary to retire to forest to achieve this goal. It is here and now that we can work for its attainment. If this ultimate aim is kept in view, all our actions will be marked by righteousness and life will become a divine play and a continuous divine service. Our mind and senses will become our friends and helpers. 'There is nothing good or bad but thinking makes it so'. God has not made anything useless or evil. It is the motive and the use we make of any object and organ that make them good or bad.

Motive is the guiding principle of all actions and comes from the ultimate purpose of life in view. Anger and passion are not bad if they are used at an appropriate time for accomplishment of nobler purpose. Anger can become righteous indignation and passion a means to bring higher soul on earth. Wealth can remove the sorrow and sufferings of the poor and the needy. Man will not stoop to foul means to achieve wealth or success. The same thing done at the same time with different motives will carry different value and result. It is the philosophy of this attitude towards life that is stressed by the Bhagavad Gita and other scriptures. Actions will bring about liberation rather than bondage. Actions are performed by all, saints and sinners, *Yogis* and *Bhogis*, but the difference lies in their attitude and understanding. One man lives and works for the sake of others, using his organs as his servants for carrying out the behests of the Soul, and the other lives for gratification of his senses, as a slave of mind and body, and works for his own pleasures and comforts even at the cost of others! Though both perform actions the difference is great and material. By adopting a selfish attitude one never attains happiness and learns the lesson by going through costly and bitter experiences of many births, bearing avoidable sufferings and sorrows!

Its what you think that makes the world
Seem dull or bright to you.
Your mind may colour all things gray
Or make them radiant hue.
Be glad today, be true and wise,
Seek gold amid the dross;
Waste neither time nor thought about
The bridge you'll never cross.
There's useful work for you to do
With hand and brain and heart;
There's urgent human service, too
In which to take your part.
Make every opportunity
A gain and not a loss;
The best is yours, so do not fear
The bridge you'll never cross.

G.Kleisiser

2

THE PRACTICE OF DIVINE LIFE*

O Lord, our Lord,
How majestic is thy name in all the earth!
When I look at thy heavens, the work of thy fingers,
The moon, the stars which thou hast established.
What is man, that thou are mindful of him ?
Yet thou hast made him little less than God,
And dost crown him with glory and honour.
Thou hast given him dominion over the works of thy hands, Thou hast put all things under his feet.

P.S.-VII

According to the anthropologists,[1] the evolution of man (*homo sapiens*) was from an early ape, particularly from chimpanzee or gorilla.

The first pedestrian on the road to *homo sapiens* was *proconsul*, considered to be of very early ape who lived 25 million years ago. It is now certain that the present species of *homo sapiens* has been living for at least 25,000 years. This species includes the whole of mankind.

There are many theories but the more modern view is that man is in existence on earth for several million years.

In 1971-72 Richard Leady, an American anthropologist, found a skull near Lake Rudlof in Kenya, which is said to be 20,50,000 years old. If that is the true age of the skull, this skull would be about a million years older than any other fossil of man so far discovered. As the skull, according to Leady, is different from all the skulls of early man so far found, it is but natural to maintain that it does not fit in with any of the present theories of evolution. The brain of this skull is not only large, but has a close resemblance with the skull of modern man.

Recently Dr. Russel L. Ciochan[1] of the University of North Carolina

---

* First Prize Essay—*Divine Life*, April, 1942 (Revised and enlarged).

1. *Animal Biology* by Mr. E.H. Jordan, *Science Today*, March, 1976.

said that the bone fragments of lower jaw found in Burma suggest that the higher primates, the ancestors of ape and of man, may have developed 40 million years ago, that is 10 million years earlier than so far believed.

Man's cranium (brain cavity) increased from 615 cc to 1450 cc during the period of about 17,50,000 years.[2]

From the survey of brain weights from 1860 to 1940 it was found that male human brain registered an increased average weight from 1372 grammes to 1424 grammes, while female brain showed an increase from 1242 to 1265 grammes.[3]

Prof. J.A.N. Corsellis of the Department of Neuropathology at the Institute of Psychiatry in London and Dr. A.K.H. Miller of the Department of Neuropathology at Runwell Hospital in Essex (U.K.), who together conducted the study, pointed out that the weight of women's brain remained static between 1860 and 1900. Since 1900 it has shown annual increase of 0.62 grammes which is slightly lower than the corresponding figure for male, which is 0.66 grammes a year.

Mr. J.B. Lippincott writes in *Basic Physiology and Anatomy* that size of brain is not indicative of intelligence.

Cerebral substance is said to have more than 12,000 million cells, which are connected with each other by fibres.

Man as a species has made a great leap in secular knowledge; naturally provision of growth is inherent in man.

It is not only man who is undergoing gradual and slow evolution, even plants, animals and minerals are under slow process of atomic evolution. Man has achieved his physical perfection, cul-de-sac. His further evolution can now be spiritual as his consciousness can flower to perfection only in Universal Consciousness.

The above claim of anthropologists about the origin of man and his evolution through ages is at variance with the belief of some religions. But, according to Hindu *Puranas* (specially *the Vishnu Purana*), which are archaic records of mankind , Manusmriti and Vedas, creation was in four stages: (i) Sarga, relating to the origin of Akasa and birth of the five Tattvas (ii) In Pratisarga stage, stars, planets, sun, moon, earth and oceans were created and life started in water, (iii) Srishti, this stage commenced with the origin of plants, vegetable life on earth, then reptiles and mammals came into being and finally man appeared. (iv)

1. *The Hindustan Times*, dated 13-7-1979.
2. *Animal Biology* by E.L. Jorden.
3. *Science Today*, November, 1977.

In fourth stage different peoples and races were formed due to climatic and geographical variations on earth.

Whatever may have been the case about the evolution of man on this planet, it has been his experience that he is always striving for something or the other to be cheerful and happy. As the time goes on, he makes himself more and more comfortable. He has acquired many things; he starting from stone weapons, has now developed atomic, hydrogen bombs; from caves and huts he has constructed flats, buildings for his living. He has made all types of furniture, appliances, gadgets and computers. He manufactures finest wine to drink, various types of delicious foods to eat, marries many beautiful women to comfort him. He manufactures finest cloth to wear, accumulates gold, precious stones, diamonds, rubies and so on, to decorate himself and his consorts.

Sophisticated air-conditioned cars, aeroplanes are made for easy and convenient transport and conveyance. Many scientific inventions, of course, wonderful inventions like electricity, radio, telephone and television have added to his comforts and powers. He physically reached the moon. All this material progress has been achieved and is still continuing. His struggle has been continuing for ages and there appears to be no end. The more comforts he acquires, the more 'wanting' he feels.

Despite all this, he has not achieved permanent happiness from the worldly things and comforts. Body's needs are few and can be met, but desires, which are generated in his mind are endless and recurring. When one's desire is fulfilled, another raises its head and this process goes on *ad infinitum*. Satisfaction and happiness recede from the sight like a mirage or like a musk deer running in search of fragrance which is really coming out from its own body.

Guru Nanak says: "Unhappy is the world," and the Buddha concludes, "Life is fraught with sufferings." Galib, the great Urdu poet, says:

kaid-a hayat wa bande gum asal main dono aik hein,
maut say pahlay admi gum say nijat paaye kyon?

(Life and sorrow are wedded together; how can a man free himself from sorrow before his death?)

I asked the bud of a flower,
You grow to smile once in life
The bud said, 'O man, in this
world, who gets even one smile ?'

> Whatever pleasures are born of contacts (with objects) are only sources of sorrow; they have a beginning and end, O Son of Kunti (Arjuna) no wise man delights in them.
>
> *Bhagavad Gita*, V.22

Sigmund Freud carried out research for over 40 years on human mind and came to the conclusion that man as such cannot be happy. If he is not unhappy that is sufficient. Eastern sages and seers, who have not only studied mind and its mysteries but have gone beyond it, say that man can be happy not by falling down to the level of animals, but going beyond mind, with awareness.

The structure of human society is basically pleasure-seeking. From early childhood to death, man, knowingly or unknowingly, is trying to find it and retain it, but disappointment sets him thinking why he is not always happy. Why is there death, sickness, sorrow, poverty, separation? Where all his struggle, hopes, fears, joys lead him? Sooner or later he realizes that worldly pleasures, however great they may be, are ephemeral and transitory. They will not give him everlasting peace which he craves for. The worldly joys are intermixed with pain, sorrow, anxieties, tribulations and sufferings. Pleasures cannot be separated from sufferings like positive and negative poles of a magnet.

He also finds that in this world things move in circle and there is nothing stationary. One who is born must die one day. From a seed a plant grows, blooms and completes its journey by yielding seed.

Stars and planets come out of nebulae and ultimately go back unto the nebulae. The universe is expanding, stars are being formed and disintegrated, some sucked through a Black Hole. This Law of Cyclicality can equally apply to other small and big things, plants, animals and to man also. He has come out of God (call 'That' by any name, viz Nature, Absolute or Brahman) and has ultimately to return to God to complete the circle. (See illustration.)

To understand the cause of man's unhappiness, to solve the riddle of life and the Law of Cyclicality, the need for religion arose. The word 'religion' has been derived from the Latin word, 're' meaning again and 'ligare' meaning to join together, to join the individual soul to the Universal Soul. Man has forgotten his real source which is characterised by Existence, Knowledge and Bliss and is, therefore, in trouble. To be happy he must realise the real source again, and complete the mission in this world.

Religion is the manifestation of Divinity already within man. It is

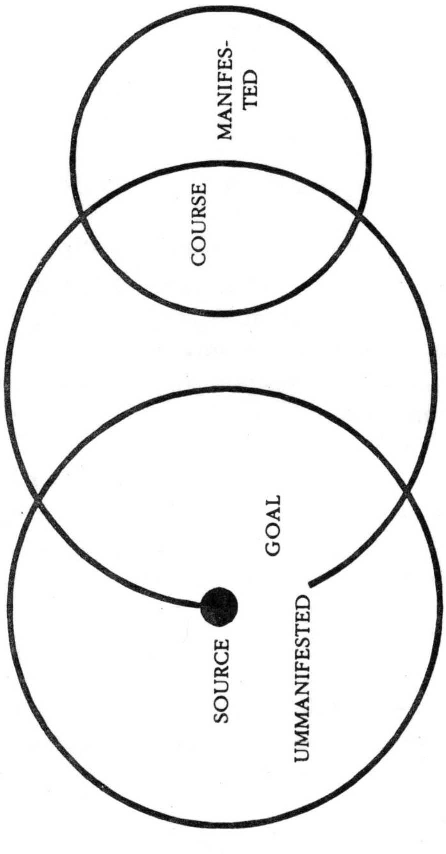

Law of Cyclicality
(From Fullness to Fullness)

perception and realization of one's true self. Religion is love—it is deep melting into existence. It gives us steadiness of mind and everlasting peace. It teaches the art of human relationship and art of living.

Unfortunately, history is full of instances where people have waged wars, committed violence and crimes in the name of religion. They have shed more blood for it than for gaining material and territorial benefits. But such people who have fought and are fighting in the name of religion, have been in the dark and are still groping in ignorance. Terrorists who murder innocent people or kill to take revenge are misguided youths. They are setting in motion a vicious circle, which is dangerous and harmful for all. Violence and retaliation are not preached but condemned by all religions.

The essentials of all religions are the same. The paths are different, but the goal is one. They all converge to a central point in the end. Paths have to be different because there are different individual temperaments, tastes, inclinations, circumstances, different countries, people with their own traditions, history, customs and due to climatic and geographical variations.

A study of the religions of the world will reveal a thread of unity in all of them. As all human beings are essentially the same in blood, bone, emotions and thinking, so all religions are basically the same and aim at the salvation of man, admitting the presence of some Supreme Power, of Principle, of Personal God, who is believed to control this vast limitless universe, beyond human imagination. This underlying truth has been discovered and verified by many seers and sages. In recent past Sri Ramakrishna Paramahamsa, who practised many types of sadhanas under Hinduism, Islam and Christianty, realised the same result. Besides many others late, J . Krishnamurthi, a great thinker and philosopher of modern age, stresses the fundamental truth of all basic philosophies.

No religion on earth preaches violence, immorality, or misconduct. When an aspirant and a new convert of Jewish faith came to Hillel, a Jewish sage who lived 2000 years ago, and asked him to teach the essence of Judaism in nutshell and in a moment, Hillel replied, "That which is hateful unto thee, do not do unto the neighbour. This is the whole of the Torah." Christ said, "Love thy neighbour", and similar teachings are found in all religions.

Religion starts from Faith; science from doubt and logic. Science is concerned with the known and religion with the unknown.

Several so-called saints and gurus have come up in recent years, making tall claims and doing business of religion. They are misleading simple people. Their aim is to make money, to enjoy all comforts at the cost of the people. They are not religious they are opportunists, hypocrites deceiving others for their selfish ends or for the sake of money. Everyone is aware that good and bad are both present together in this world. Like a rajahamsa (King Swan), who separates milk from water, as the saying goes, one has to distinguish between a true Master and a charlatan.

No other subject is so much misunderstood, misinterpreted and misused as religion. Religion is not a cloak to be worn on a particular day, as Shelly says, or it is not "the opium for the people," as interpreted by Karl Marx. It does not consist in observing rituals, wearing certain types of clothes or smearing the body with ash or sandalwood paste or living in forest or going to temple, mosque or church. It is not a book to be read and then to be preserved on the shelf of an almirah.

Religion is something real, something to be practised in daily living. It is an art of daily living, living with others, living with one's own self in discipline. It is not escaping the suffering, but living with it. It is not compensation for what you lack in life. Its real aim is not attaining siddhis or doing certain secret practices to harm others or to gain money or reputation. It is basically to create an ecstatic life—a life full of bliss, harmony, accord, sincerity and service. An animal enjoys pleasure of senses, a wise man takes delight in his intellect and an advanced aspirant in his spiritual ecstasy, or derives joy from his selfless service to humanity.

Religion teaches man that if he wants to be happy in this world of sorrows, he must understand himself , control his lower nature which he inherited from the past, make best use of his senses, realising his mastery, supremacy over the sense-organs and directing and guiding his energies into proper channels. He is like a driver of a chariot drawn by ten horses. He is a master, rider and not servant of horses (senses). He is controlling the chariot—his body.

> "For a yogi whose mind is perfectly calm, who is sinless, whose passion is subdued and who is identified with Brahman, supreme happiness comes."
>
> *Bhagavad Gita*, V.27

To gain control of mind is a great achievement. Nothing is difficult for a person who has achieved mastery over his mind, because mind makes his world.

Control of mind is achieved through constant practice, renunciation, leading a regular *sattvika* and divine life.

Shri Ekanath says that there are three methods to achieve control of mind, namely, (*i*) to treat the mind as an enemy and kill it, (*ii*) to treat it as a friend and befriend it, and (*iii*) to ignore it.

Other suggestion is to keep the mind constantly engaged. Psychologists advise us to control the shift of attention rather than to control the attention from shifting as on a cycle you cannot remain standing still but you can direct the movement of the cycle, to stand on it.

Essentials of Divine life are described in the *Bhagavad Gita* (XVI.1-3) as under:

> Fearlessness, purity of mind, steadfastness in the yoga of wisdom, alms-giving, self-restraint and sacrifice, study of the scriptures, austerity and straightforwardness, (XVI.1).
>
> Harmlessness, truth, absence of wrath, renunciation, peacefulness, absence of bearing tales, compassion to living beings, uncovetousness, mildness, modesty, absence of restiveness, (XVI.2).
>
> Vigour, forgiveness, fortitude, purity, absence of enmity and pride—these are the qualities of a human being who is born with divine properties, O Bharata (XVI.3).

Man is divine by nature, but by force of his past deeds (*samskaras*), he has forgotten his real being. Ultimately he has to unite with the Supreme, as he came out of Him, so has to return unto Him, to complete the circle.

As man works hard to acquire secular education, and toils from morning to evening to earn his livelihood, so he has also to make efforts to remove the veil of ignorance, so that he may recognise the qualities which are already present in him. He who desires to rise, evolve and to elevate himself has to do something and undo something as is explained in the following pages. Little is gained by verbal discussion and vain imagination. One has to act and live in the present and should obey the commands of inner voice, ever urging man to right action and right direction.

> The grace of the conscious light, upon the apparent self (jiva), fulfills itself in an impulsion from inner urge or compulsion from without.
>
> *Sat Darshana Bhashya—Ramana Maharshi*

I may mention that in India and in other developing countries people are worried and occupied most of the time about earning their livelihood. There is unemployment and poverty among the masses. When they are not able to meet their basic needs (i.e. food, clothing and shelter), how can they be expected to turn to spiritual path? At the same time it has also been observed that those who are in trouble turn towards God more quickly than those in affluence. While riches seem to corrupt a person, poverty too can be a hindrance in his progress in life.

Everyone has to work in the right way for the betterment of his circumstances. Wherever he is placed in life by birth or by circumstances, he has to lift himself up as a true Karma Yogi by his righteous actions, courage and good behaviour, and always by remembering the Supreme Power residing in his heart. If he perseveres, a good time will be coming, as after night, morning surely comes.

As soon as we get real craving for spiritual uplift, God sends a guide. No sooner is the disciple ready, than the Master appears and we shall know the *Sadhana* (method) suitable to our taste, temperament and bent of mind. Success in any *sadhana* depends upon the following preliminaries which are like preparing the ground for sowing the seed.

3

PREPARATION FOR INWARD JOURNEY

GOOD HEALTH

नायमात्मा बलहीनेन लभ्यः

Unhappiness and ill health go together

(*Mundaka Upanishad* 111.2-4)

tangdasti agar na ho Galib,
tandursti hazar niamat hai

(If there is no poverty, health is a great blessing)

(Galib)

You should possess good health for success in every sphere of life. You cannot do anything without being in good health. Body is a gross vehicle of soul and has to be kept fit and fine.

Disease means 'dis -ease'. It is a condition in which the rhythm is broken in your inner bio-energy. *Svasthya* literally means 'to be oneself'. You cannot be yourself when you are ill, as your attention is brought again and again to your ailing body or to the part of it which is ailing. Health means to be whole. A healthy person is whole and also holy and his energy moves in a rhythmic way, in a circle, which represents perfection. A perfectly healthy person is neither sensual nor sexual, as he enjoys his health and is happy within himself. Good health is essential to make life worth living and for achievement of our goal in life.

For acquiring good health you have to take care of your diet. It should be wholesome, fresh, pleasant and nourishing. It should preferably consist of fruits, green vegetables, salad, juices, soups, dry fruits, milk, cheese, butter, bran, and sprouted grains. You should avoid fried foods, too much fat, spices, chillies, sugar and salt. Liquid vegetable oil (fat) helps to prevent cholesterol in the arteries, while animal fats promote its deposits.

You should not over-eat, rather keep a little space inside your stomach. The diet should be balanced in its contents, viz. carbohydrates, fats, proteins, vitamins and minerals.

You can judge your bodily system and should eat what suits you according to place, country, position and heredity.

You must masticate each morsel of food in your mouth. Do not use intestines in place of your teeth.

If you are practising yoga, or are engaged in spiritual activities, you should avoid *tamasika* food, i.e. meat*, wine and smoking or any sort of intoxicants . Night meals should be light and taken two hours before going to bed.

The second requirement is daily exercise. It can be yoga asanas, morning walk, surya namaskar** or any game or sport. Sun bath, and oil massage of the body during winter are recommended. Those who follow some spiritual sadhana should do yogic asanas. Yogic asanas strengthen inner parts of the body.

The third requirement is physical and mental relaxation. The physical body of man is so ordained by nature that every organ has its time for recuperation, but you ignore it by over-working your organs and nerves. If you are tense or worried you cannot be healthy. Most of the diseases are caused by your wrong mental attitudes, anger, greed, jealousy, passion and so on. A famous Soviet scientist and photographer, Semyon Davidonch Kirlian has been able to photograph aura of a person, his energy-body (plasma body). By the study of this auric photograph, serious illness, which may attack a person in future, can be revealed many months in advance.

Fundamentally a physical illness is first foreshadowed in the mental sphere. From the lines on your hand and the shape and condition of your nails, a palmist can tell about your health in advance, as an astrologer can tell about illness from the position of stars in your horoscope. It is, therefore, most important to keep your mind at peace. It is not work that tires a person, it is the worry.

---

* It is discovered by experiment that meat abstainers have more endurance than meat eaters.

Dr. McCollum, the discoverer of Vitamins A and D, says:

"I have not the slightest hesitation in saying that a vegetarian diet, supplemented with fairly liberal amount of milk, is the most satisfactory diet that man can take... All the evidence from both animal experimentation and human experience supports, in a manner which can never be broken down, the viewpoint that meat is not necessary in the human diet."

** Read Ten Points to Health by Sri Balasahib Pandit Pratinidhi, Raja of Audh.

Finally, you should have good sleep at night. Sleep is unconscious and compulsory relaxation. All living beings and even Devas (Gods) want to enjoy sleep. During sleep the body mechanism is engaged in repair work. It has been found scientifically that an average person, consciously or unconsciously, spends more time in dreams than in sound sleep during night. Dream is the preserver of sleep. Dreams are useful as they give vent to our unfulfilled desires and injured emotions.

For ordinary ailments, you can cure yourself by change in diet or by taking some homely herbal treatment rather than resorting to strong antibiotic drugs.

To conclude, you should have a scientific approach to the needs of the body. You cannot expect Divinity to shine through a sickly, unhealthy and unclean body.

GOOD CONDUCT

Vimala Thakar says:

> "Life is movement in relationship and divinity is phenomenon of inter-relationship of everything that exists and moves in this universe."

Your behaviour in and outside your house should be harmonious, cheerful and helpful. It should not in any way harm others through word, thought or deed. 'Do to others as you wish to be done by' is the golden principle.

You should be regular and punctual in discharge of your duties. You should not lose your temper and should keep balance of mind at all costs and consequences. Remember: "Evenness of mind is yoga."

You should keep your things in order and in a good arrangement, as disorder in a living room creates mental distraction and inconvenience.

You should be watchful of your speech. Speech is an energy. Chhandogya Upanishad says, "Speech is Tejomaya."

Therefore, you should not speak that which you do not understand, intend or imply, or which injures the feelings of others.

You should keep silence for a whole day once a week or month.

You should also try to complete what you once decided to do. There should be no procrastination due to lack of favourable circumstances, which may not be available, as in this uncertain world something or the other may be going wrong most of the time. So you may not be able to get 100% congenial atmosphere or environment to pursue your aim.

When you are suffering from anger or greed, your behaviour becomes irritable and improper towards your family and fellow beings. Modern psychologists have discovered them as unnatural traits. When any person insults you or causes any provocation, you should wait and take at least seven breaths before you answer him or take any action on his provocation. Actually anger spreads poison in the blood and debars clear thinking. It makes the mind restless and wastes energy.

If you watch the face of an angry person, you will know the ugliness of anger. He may be trembling. His face will get red. He will begin to breathe rapidly. His eyes will be burning, and so on. So be careful about anger overtaking you. Nothing should be done in a fit of anger. Similarly greed leads man to difficult situation. It is said ill-gotten is ill-spent. It is actual experience of many that only honest earnings can give real satisfaction and remain faithful to the earner. His children generally do not spoil his hard- earned money.

BRAHMACHARYA

ब्रह्मचर्यप्रतिष्ठायां वीर्यलाभः ॥

By establishment of Brahmacharya, energy is gained.

Yoga Sutra, II.38

ब्रह्मचर्येण तपसा देवाः मृत्युमपाघ्नत ॥

The Devas (Gods) conquered death by the penance of Brahmacharya.

Atharva Veda

Brahmacharya literally means "discipline for the attainment of knowledge" or constantly thinking of Brahman or God. In broad sense, it denotes purity of character, purity of thought, word and deed. It means mastery over the senses, particularly over the sex force, as by the control of sex all other organs are brought automatically under control. The preservation of this vital energy is most essential for health, happiness and progress. It is the most important virtue to keep strong, healthy and active for a longer period of life.

Brahmacharya (celebacy) is an important step towards God-realization. This is the foundation of yoga and this chapter is meant for those who want to tread the path of yoga or want to maintain good health till old age.

It is not for those who are interested in sex and whose aim is limited to the enjoyment of the body.

The practice of celebacy, for which the term Brahmacharya is used here, invigorates and strengthens body, nerves and mind. It rebuilds the cells and tissues. It bestows natural beauty and artificial aids and make-up becomes superfluous. It gives power and resists fatigue and disease. It enables a person to face difficulties in the daily struggle of life. Loss of semen results in irritability and anger in temperament. Semen is the seed of man. It is the seed that develops into a tree. It is *bindu* (point) that develops into lines, letters, words, sentences, and books. Semen is the source of life. Many insects die after sexual intercourse. One sex act releases 120 calories of heat, which is equal to the heat produced after running fast for a mile, or the amount of energy spent in physical labour for ten days, or mental work performed during three days.

Excessive loss of semen spreads disease and disaster in the body. There is a very well known English saying: "If wealth is lost, nothing is lost; if health is lost, something is lost, but if character is lost, everything is lost." Semen is atomic energy in man. One spermatozoon is capable of producing one human being, while millions are lost at one time. Semen is animal magnetism, the lustre, the brilliance, the intelligence and memory, the storehouse of vitality, the aid to longevity and the basis of strong will power. Man is not man without it. If he violates the laws of nature, he degrades himself to the lower level more than that of the animals, who meet only in their respective mating seasons and not after the conception of females.

Celebacy can be practised by all, according to the stages of life. A student's position is quite different from that of a married person, or from an elderly retired person. A student must conserve and preserve his sex-energy for his studies and ultimately for the future marital life. Napolean Hill in his book, *Think and Grow Rich*, has mentioned that sex-energy can be transmuted for higher creative purposes of science, art, poetry, etc. and that it can help a person in developing his/her sixth sense.

A married person can enjoy reasonably. An elderly person can utilize this energy for the preservation of his health from deterioration and for higher purposes of life. When a person is healthy, he does not indulge in sex, he indulges in love, human or spiritual. Sex is superfluous energy. It is a safety valve. If the energy used for sexual enjoyment be transformed inwardly, human body can be preserved for any length of time.

By the establishment of celebacy vigour is gained.

Yoga Sutra

He who is without desire, says a Chinese classic, has an insight into the secret essence.

If a society permits free sex, it will perish like the cultures of Rome and Greece.

Brahmacharya does not only mean abstaining from eight forms of sexual indulgence, but it includes purification and awakening of consciousness. In a wider sense, Brahmacharya is attained when duality disappears from consciousness and one Supreme Power is seen everywhere (Brahman). In sexual pleasure also a person loses the sense of duality.

As the vital fluid is *bindu* (centre of the physical body), similarly life, mind and *vijnana* (discrimination), which together constitute the subtle body, have each a *bindu* in their respective centres. Vital force is connected with mind and mind with bindu. In observing celebacy, bindu is stabilised and starts its upward journey, which is known as awakening of Kundalini. It ultimately meets *maha bindu* in the pericarp of the *thousand-petalled lotus*. Unless *bindu* rises above the navel point, it is not free from the law of gravity. Mahayana Cult of Buddhism also prescribes some fine natural methods of purification of *bindu*.

Brahmacharya (celebacy) is meant for both man and woman, as each one of them has male and female harmones. Generally man reaches orgasm earlier than woman and hence greater control for men is advised.

Mahavira says, unless you go beyond sex you cannot be free from the cycle of birth and death. Buddhism also attaches much importance to Brahmacharya in its code of conduct or *sila sampat*. Jain and other religions also give similar importance to it.

The path of the Karmayogi, or of an ideal householder *(Gribastha)*, is as difficult as that of a yogi in a Himalayan cave. So his status is superior to other ashramas, as all other ashramas depend on the householder. It is comparatively easy to remain aloof from the world and practice self-control rather than to live, mingle and work daily among the sense objects and then to exercise restraint. Poverty is not renunciation, as impotence is not sex control. If a married man visits his beloved wife for the sake of maintaining the line of progeny, he is as good a celebate as an ascetic who observes perfect vow of celebacy.

The growth of population* in our country is said to be to the tune of 33000 every day. If this increase in population continues, the future of the country cannot be bright.

This growth has already caused a problem and concern to the country. All progress is nullified. Production and development cannot keep pace with the birth-rate. Unemployment is growing and educated people are without jobs. Married couples in urban and rural areas have to exercise control, either natural self-restraint or scientific birth control. They should keep within reasonable limits so as to be able to live and educate their children properly. It is of no use to produce children when one is not able to bring them up properly, feed or educate them and make them useful citizens of the country. Otherwise they will be a burden to the parents, to society and will disrupt the economic condition of their family and ultimately of their country.

To curb population growth, abortion has been legalised by the government in India. It is simplified by modern medical science, but it has given freedom to the youngsters to indulge in premarital sex or stray sex. Vulgar cinema songs and blue films have added fuel to the fire. Morality and chastity have been lowered. Therefore, moral teachings in colleges and schools should be introduced and given proper importance. Moral standard and its value should be raised and praised in society.

Formation and Importance of Semen

If we just reflect upon the formation of semen inside human body, we can very well realize its importance and value.

According to the Ayurvedic system of medicine, the food that we eat is transformed into chyle, chyle gets converted into blood, from blood is produced flesh, flesh produces fat, fat is transformed into bone, bone forms the marrow and the marrow at last produces semen. Still further semen is sublimated into *ojas* and from *ojas* intellect is formed. Thus it is clear from the above process that semen is the finest essence of what we take in. It is the essence of essences or the butter churned out of foodstuff taken through mouth and so is the most precious substance. It is said that 60 drops of butter make one drop of blood and 60 drops of blood make one drop of semen.

The modern medical sciences regard semen as combined secretion of the testicles, the seminal vesicles, prostrate, Cowper's and mucus producing glands of urethra. The most important content of semen is spermatozoa in addition to its various contents. Spermatozoa are formed in the form of the germ cells of testicles. Persons suffering from defects

---

* The present population is estimated at 800.00 millions (1987).

in semen are quite likely to develop sexual neurasthenia or may become hypochondriacs or mentally defective.

It has been discovered that most valuable cells in human organism are germ cells and the aging process reaches them last of all. Sri Swami Sivananda in his book on the Practice of Brahmacharya, quotes Dr. E.P. Miller as under:

> "All waste of spermatic secretions, whether voluntary or involuntary, is a direct waste of life force. It is almost universally conceded that the choicest elements of blood enter into the composition of the spermatic secretion."

Science has also confirmed intimate relationship between semen and mind. It is found that the 90% of all the potency troubles are not of physical but of psychological character. This is truly supported by the fact that the diseases carried by parents are transferred to their offsprings, in addition to features and characteristics.

Gopi Krishna, writing about Kundalini Yoga, says that real food for nervous system is bio-plasma, an essence from sex glands which ascends via spinal cord up to the brain.

Difficulties on the Path

Self-restraint is not as easy as it is thought to be. It is most difficult to practice. Sex plays most important role in human life since birth. Its mastery is the biggest achievement. If a person controls his tongue (eating, speaking) and his sex, he can perform miracles. Had it been easy to control sex it would have lost all the value and precious quality. Precious thing is always scarce and rare and high achievements are difficult, and therefore demand much greater effort. But it is the bravest man who surmounts obstacles and goes ahead. Perseverance overcomes mountains.

In the present day difficulties have increased due to the advent of the cinema, multiplication of wants, cheap and obscene and low-rate novels and reading material, filthy advertisements and wild imitation of the West in food and fashion. Unless the government and people cooperate together, improvement is not possible. The Cinema, TV and VCR have many good points, but have no doubt exerted some unhealthy influence also on immature minds and uneducated manual workers.

Cinemas generally present an imperfect and unrealistic picture of life. It is argued that the producers have to look to the public taste and demand to earn profits. The pictures of sober themes or pictures devoid of sex and violence, have been financial failures and none can afford to lose money on unproductive enterprises. After a hard day's work people like relaxation and not moral lessons. In the heat of the arguments we forget that taste can be refined. We can aid in the cultivation of healthy tastes by providing good entertainment in several ways. The Government, the writers, the producers, all can unite to raise the taste and level of films, radio, T.V. and the cinema, the easy, speedy, and popular means of mass uplift. Special educative and informative films can be produced for students and children. Something has been promised to be done recently in this regard.

Psychology of cinema has been explained by Mr. A.E. Mander in his book, *Psychology for Everyman andWoman*, in these words:

> "Clearly it is because by identifying oneself with the character of the story on the screen, one is able to gratify by 'proxy' some 'want' which is unsatisfied in real life."

Music is the food of the soul and it is intended to uplift man to higher realms of consciousness to invoke devotion and love. Love, beauty and art have their own importance in life, but vulgarity and indecency cannot be permitted. It is of no use imitating the West in all matters. India has its own ancient and rich culture and civilization, which have stood the test of times and which have to be protected.

We can learn many good things from the West, but cannot afford to follow them blindly and lose our sublimity of thought and spiritual aims.

Marriage among Hindus and other communities, is considered ideal and sacred and great stress is laid on chastity, purity and its continuity for the whole life.

Many bad customs have crept into society; and the result of all this has been that several marriages are broken for want of mutual adjustment. Some people have made marriage a business affair and many hearts are bleeding and murders are committed of innocent brides for greed.

Aids to Celebacy

If we truly realise and understand the glory and importance of celebacy, several methods can be employed to practice it.

The pleasure in sex comes from the self. When we realise this, sex will drop. An understanding should be created by which sex drops by itself. Sex is the lowest short-lived ecstasy.

Fighting with sexual desires will dissipate more energy than indulgence in sex. Transformation of mind is a positive effort, whereas suppression is a negative one. A forcible suppression and repression cause division and lower the strength. We have to go beyond sex and look inside for the source from where the desire is coming.

We have to change our outlook towards sex and it will lead us to success. Woman can be a mother, a sister or a daughter. She is the incarnation of Shakti (the manifest power of the Unseen). We should have a chaste look, good company of persons and books. Lord Jesus says, "If you have a lustful look, you have already committed adultery in your heart."

When we look consciously and in totality at the face of a woman, we see nature's beauty, and lust does not enter.

It is always an indolent mind or hand that finds some mischief to do. Keeping oneself busy is an excellent method to attain success in self-restraint. Further, there should be some mental background to fall back upon when there are some leisurely moments. That background may be solving of any business proposition, planning for the day, or repetition of Divine name or thinking of nature's beauty.

Mind, *prana* (breath) and semen (*virya*) are connected together. The mind is to be controlled and disciplined. Undesirable thoughts have to be replaced by desirable ones. It is to be followed on the basis of the experiences of those who have gone ahead of us. A young bachelor or spinster, who has been celebate or chaste, can really enjoy married life, and the couple who exercise self-restraint during marital life, are capable of enjoying sex till late in life. When there is gap, crystallisation of love happens, and pleasure of sexual enjoyment is enhanced.

Advanced students of yoga and those who wish to accomplish something worthwhile in the world or those who want to rise above the average level of humanity, have to conserve this vital energy for higher purpose and for superior and longer happiness. A bachelor should remain pure and a married man should look upon his wife as a companion, co-worker or equal partner in life's struggle and not as an instrument of sexual enjoyment or as a domestic worker. It is advisable for such aspirants to sleep in separate rooms, as temptation overcomes a person by degrees. One goes on slipping step by step till one reaches the extreme end of the precipice of the hill of passion to fall into the abyss of inordinate lust. Cause and rise of the sex desire should, therefore, be nipped in the bud by a change in direction, so that it does not spread further like an infectious disease and take hold of one's consciousness.

Life has to be made regular and punctual. 'Early to bed and early to rise makes a man healthy, wealthy and wise,' is a grand motto to be followed. *Sattvika food**, like pure fresh milk, butter, fresh fruit, green vegetables, dry fruits, almonds, sugarcane and honey are helpful to a great extent, while highly seasoned dishes, fried food, chillies, meat, fish, egg, tobacco, liquors or other intoxicants, bitter things, over-ripe fruits and excessive salt and sugar, heavy meals at night are harmful.

Cold bath, hip bath, morning exercise in open and fresh air, yogic asanas (postures) such as sarvangasana, bhujangasana, matsyasana, surya namaskara, are helpful.

Sex is a very vast subject and beyond the scope of this book. We will, however, do well to remember Socrates' famous advice to his disciples and try to invoke divine grace with devotion and repetition of His name for guiding us across the formidable sea of passion.

Bhagavan Ramana Maharshi says in *Hymns to Arunachala*, "Save me from the cruel snares of fascinating women and honour me with Thyself, O Arunachala."

---

* It is a fallacy to think that *Sattvika* food is poor. On the other hand, recent laboratory tests have shown that this is the best diet for potency. The following rules to promote potency are given in the *Encyclopaedia of Sexual Knowledge*, Volume II by Drs. A. Willy, L. Vander, C. Fisher and others.

(1) Purification of blood of acids by abstaining from meat, cured foods, bacon and fish.
(2) Diet of vegetables, fruits, nuts and wholemeal bread.
(3) Use of food containing vitamin E.
(4) Spices and eroticising foods to be avoided.
(5) Alchohol, nicotine, coffee, and tea to be eliminated.

It has been proved by laboratory tests that spermatozoa of inveterate drunkards, even when they are still fertile, are literally poisoned and cannot possibly develop into a sane and normal being. Prof. Morel in his essay, "Physical, Intellectual and Moral Degeneracy of the Human Race' established the following table on alcoholic heredity:

1st Generation—Immorality, brutality, depravity.
2nd Generation—Hereditary drunkenness, fits, general paralysis etc.
3rd Generation—Sobriety, tendency of hypochondria, homicidal tendency etc.
4th Generation—Under-developed intelligence, stupidity, transition to idiocy, and finally probable extinction of the line.

CONCENTRATION (Dharana) (Key to Success)

"Fixation of mind on any object is called Dharana"

Yoga Sutra, III.1

"The difference between an ordinary mind and the mind of a Newton consists principally in this that one is capable of the application of more continuous attention than the other."

— *Sir William Hamilton*

Concentration is focussing of the mind on a single object, without diversion. Its purpose is to fix the attention on a small field of mental vision, as mind can do only one thing at a time. This voluntary fixing of the mind on the subject in hand is to achieve its full involvement. It is the best use of the time spent. Work is accomplished efficiently without much exertion. All scientists and inventors have made inventions and discoveries by focussing the mind on a single object or point. This does not mean dwarfing and limiting the thought and activities, but is to harness the powers of mind on the work in hand. The powers of mind are intensified when all the rays are focussed on one point. It is like a rope being woven from feeble threads or like a magnifying lens which collects the rays of the sun and causes fire or small drops of rain filling rivers and causing floods.

Nothing worthwhile can be accomplished without concentration. It is the secret of all achievements and successes. Not only spiritual advancement but also worldly success is dependent upon one's capacity to concentrate. Power and quality of consciousness is at its best during the period of concentration. Extraordinary feats of Hypnotism, Mesmerism, psychic telescopy and power of travelling in subtle body, extended vision etc. are the result of deep concentration. Scientific inventions and discoveries have been possible by the power of concentration. Persons who can concentrate can also attain success in meditation and contemplation. Concentration is also the cause of pleasure or pain in our daily life.

Mind is very rebellious. It is difficult to control, or to concentrate it, as difficult as to stop the movements of a monkey. Mind's very nature is to be restless. The moment it is made to move within a given circle, it jumps and leaps and tries to cross the boundary and break limitations. If one can effectively control the mind, one can control the world. Arjuna narrated this difficulty to Lord Krishna, when he said:

> "The mind verily is, O Krishna, restless, turbulent, strong and unyielding. I deem it quite as difficult to control as the wind". (VI.34)

The blessed Lord replied:

> "Undoubtedly, O mighty -armed, the mind is difficult to control, and restless, but by practice, O Kaunteya, and by dispassion it can be restrained." (VI.35)

So these few words contain the kingly secret of the control of mind in nutshell. Concentration on a subject is easy if the subject is interesting and attractive to the person. Interest, attention and will are very essential to attain success in concentration and perfection will be attained by constant and regular practice in bringing the mind over and over again on the subject. Once this writer had an opportunity to place this question before Mahatma Gandhi, and his reply in his own handwriting, which is carefully preserved by me, is as under:

Dear Friend,

Concentration is attained by repeated failures and equally repeated efforts to achieve it.

Yours sincerely
M.K. GANDHI

Gandhiji laid great stress on the practice which is emphasised in Shloka 35, Chapter VI of the Bhagavad Gita. He believed that by regular and constant practice everything is possible and can be attained. It, however, does not mean struggling with the mind, but relaxing it by creating interest in the object and by persuasion.

When the subject appears uninteresting, it is because we do not understand it and do not appreciate its value. Some people can concentrate well while reading a novel or seeing any natural scenery or beauty, such as sunshine, sunset, flowers etc., but find it difficult to concentrate their mind in repeating the divine name, or in meditation. The reason is quite simple. It shows lack of intensity of desire, interest and understanding of the subject. If twenty-four hours of the day are spent in doing and thinking on a subject quite opposite to one on which we simply wish to spend a few minutes, without love or devotion, it is obviously impossible to get success in concentration. Specially in this field we want to get something for nothing.

Mind, breath (*prana*) and semen (*virya*) are related with each other. If one is controlled, the other is automatically brought under subjugation. Those who practice breath-control and celibacy, can develop strong power of concentration. When we are absorbed in some mental contemplation, our breath flows slowly and smoothly so much so that it is not felt. The number of inhalations and exhalations during a minute also decreases. While in anger and excitement, the breath flows quickly, followed by an increase in heartbeats and nervous tension. So a short-tempered and passionate person will find it difficult to concentrate. These inner distractions of anger, passion, hate, jealousy, etc. are greater and more difficult to overcome than the outer distractions of environment and noise. These outer distractions can easily be avoided, except those which are unavoidable and have to be ignored. Livingstone tells us that he did his early study amid the roar of a factory. So, one can easily habituate oneself to ignore such noise and distractions; plugging the ears with cotton and wax can be tried to stop outside noise or a secluded place can be chosen.

If we desire to attain happiness or worldly success in any undertaking, it is necessary to develop our power of concentration. We have to control the mind and make it work under our direction. We have to invoke the power which is superior to the mind—the power which enables the mind to function and gives it life and light. Concentration of mind will economise our energies. It will bring together all the forces of mind on the subject and will thus open new avenues of infinite knowledge.

I may sum up the important points on concentration in the following few lines:

(a) Think only of the subject in hand.
(b) Avoid all wasteful activities and mannerism in which some persons semi-consciously indulge, viz., shaking of hand or leg while sitting in a chair, moving mouth while writing, unconsciously repeating the same word in talk.
(c) Do not dwell again and again on the same thought or argument but try to decide after careful survey of the whole matter analysing its pros and cons.
(d) Unify your thought. If thoughts lie higgledy-piggledy in the mind, pointing to different directions, they in effect will destroy one another, like disarranged magnets, and no unification is possible .

(e) Look and think calmly. No anxiety or gasping is necessary. Remember that evenness of mind is yoga.

(f) Take interest in your work and do it wholeheartedly as a matter of duty. Remember ,work is worship and skill in action is Yoga.

(g) Control of body posture and of bodily movements, avoiding all possible distractions, is necessary to attain success.

(h) Concentration on repetition of divine name, meditation and contemplation is not the work of easy accomplishment. It requires regular and constant practice, self-confidence and control of senses. Do not be disappointed but carry on the work with perseverance and patience.

(i) Where can the mind go after all? It must return to its source, to its master! Realise your superiority over the mind.

(j) Do something which is not interesting or to your taste so that you can make the mind work according to your discretion.

(k) Try to concentrate for a limited period of time and then extend the period by and by.

(l) To drive away an unwanted thought, resort to opposite thought, e.g. to get rid of a thought of hate, think of love.

Maharshi Patanjali says:

To counteract thoughts which are inimical to Yoga, contrary thoughts should be practised. *Yoga Sutra* II.33

By following the above instructions good results are assured. Concentration of mind, of purpose, of thought and of action is the key to success in every walk of life. All successful men have worked towards their aim with one-pointedness. I will end this chapter by a quotation from Dr. Annie Beasant's famous book, *The Ancient Wisdom:*

"The student must begin by practising extreme temperance, in all things, cultivating an equable and serene state of mind; his life must be clean and his thoughts pure, his body held in strict subjection to the soul, and his mind trained to occupy itself with noble and lofty themes: he must habitually practise compassion, sympathy, helpfulness to others, with indifference to troubles and pleasures, affecting himself, and he must cultivate courage, steadfastness and devotion. Having, by persevering practice, learned to control his mind to some extent, so that he is able to keep it fixed on one line of thought for some little time, he must begin its more rigid training by a daily practice of concentration on some difficult or abstract subject, or some lofty object of devotion. This concentration means the firm fixing of the mind on one single point without wandering and without yielding to any distraction caused by external objects, by the activity of the senses, or by that of the mind itself... When it is able to hold itself thus with comparative ease, it is ready for a further step and by a strong but calm effort of the will it can throw itself beyond the highest thought it can reach while working in the physical brain, and in that effort will rise to and unite itself with the higher consciousness and find itself free of the body."

Meditation proceeds from concentration. It is expansion of attention. If concentration is a torch, meditation is like a flame.

ESSENCE OF YOGA

The word 'yoga' has been so much used and misused recently that it seems to have lost its sanctity.

The word 'yoga' is derived from the root 'yuj' meaning 'joining together'. It is the same as the word 'yoke' in English. It is transformation of human consciousness into divine consciousness.

Yoga is a method of "coming to a non-dreaming mind". It is a 'science' of being in the here and now'. It is not only a view of life, but also a way of life and a means of liberation. It is integral science of sciences

Yoga is a means of leading one to introspection, reflection and meditation. Yoga aims at making the inner experience a basis for life rather than theory or scriptures. It is an art of being. Yoga teaches order and discipline in life and actual day- to-day living. It points out your centre within. Bhagavad Gita says:

"Evenness of mind is yoga."

Maharshi Patanjali says in the *Yoga Sutra (1.2):*

"Yoga is cessation of the functioning of mind".

Mehar Baba says:

Mind stopped is God
Mind working is man
Mind slowed down is Mast *(divine ecstasy)*
Mind working fast is Mad

When there are no thoughts, a state of thoughtlessness or egolessness dawns. It is a jump into the unknown. All systems, yogas and religions have aimed at how to use the mind. To achieve this state, different methods are employed. There are four main paths to suit four main kinds of temperaments. For a man of action, for a devotional man, for a mystic or philosophical man, for a man of reason, there are Karma Yoga, Bhakti Yoga, Jnana Yoga, and Raja Yoga respectively. In Bhakti Yoga are included Japa Yoga, Mantra Yoga, Ajapa-japa, Samarpana. Similarly self-enquiry method and Vedanta are included and in Raja Yoga, Patanjali's Astanga Yoga and some other non-traditional methods are included. There are Laya Yoga, Kundalini Yoga, Turiya Yoga and Tantra Yoga which are also mentioned in the following pages. In short, I have tried not to miss any important 'Sadhana'. Sadhana comes from the root 'sadha' which means to exert or endeavour to get a particular result.

Any one system (sadhana) suitable to your taste, temperament and capacity, may be adopted. Jnana Yoga, Bhakti Yoga and Karma Yoga are not antagonistic, but are complementary. Description of all sadhanas has been given in concise and condensed form. Further details and steps can be known and enquired about as one progresses on the path.

As already explained, all Yogas (methods) or systems (Sadhanas) are aimed to dissolve the mind, to go beyond the mind, to die consciously, and to be in choiceless awareness. This is because mind is the curtain between the Self and the Supreme. The Ultimate is beyond thought and mental conception. Unless you reach the realm of silence, you are far from the entrance.

> "However men approach me, even so do I welcome them, for the paths men take from everyside is mine, O Partha".
>
> *Bhagavad Gita,* IV.11

4

KARMA YOGA

We live in deeds not in years,
In thoughts not in breaths,
In feelings, not in figures on dial.
He most lives, who thinks most,
Feels the noblest, acts the best.

Karma is a Sanskrit word which comes from the root 'Kri' meaning action. The whole universe is bound by action. There is no life without action. Every atom in the universe is involved in action. Animate and inanimate objects, consciously or unconsciously, are in action. None can refrain from performing action. Action or movement or change is the apparent character and nature of the universe and therein lies the beauty of this Eternal Play *(Lila Kshetra)*. The sun, the moon, the stars and the earth move under certain definite law and order. Every particle of even an apparently lifeless object is rotating round the centre of nucleus and thus maintains its shape and form. The vegetables grow, the rivers flow towards the sea, the flowers bloom, the wind blows, innumerable kinds of creatures take birth in the air, in the water and on the earth and die out; thus the cycle of birth and death goes on ceaselessly and indefinitely. Whence arise all actions? When did action originally start? Which came first, egg or hen? No one knows or can imagine. These are questions beyond the pale of thought. It has neither a beginning nor an end and none should waste time in worrying about the origin of things. One has to work in the living present and carry out the duties lying nearby. Man is the superior creation of the Almighty. He has been endowed with all the requisite qualities for the development of his latent powers. He has been given certain freedom of choice and intelligence for performing actions. Thus he is like a cow tied to a rope which is attached to a peg. The cow can move freely as far as the rope goes all round the peg.

There are three kinds of karmas:

Sanchita	(accumulated results of the past actions): this is the cause of character of succeeding births.
Prarabdha	(past karma which has started bearing fruit in the present birth): Such karmas are unavoidable.
Agami	karma yet to bear fruit in future.

In Karma Yoga there is four-fold attainment of (a) *Dharma* (religious merit); (b) *Artha* (wealth); (c) *Kama* (satisfaction of desires), and (d) *Moksha* (liberation).

The theory of reincarnation has now been proved by evidence and instances verified by research scholars all over the world. Without accepting this theory, you cannot explain the differences, disparities, analogies found everywhere in the world.

Actions have been allocated to man according to his station in life and stage of evolution. The greatest authority on Karma Yoga in Hindu religion is the Bhagavad Gita, which reveals the splendid and supreme secrets of the Yoga of Action. Its message is for mankind and its teachings have universal application, especially in the present age (Kali-yuga) when the people have complexity, tension and mechanical living. It is the most scientific and an unparalleled work on the law of Action as Patanjali's Yoga-sutra is on Yoga.

The span of life is divided into four stages: *Brahmacharya* (student life), *Grihastha* (married life), *Vanaprastha* (period of preparation for the attainment of knowledge of the Self) and *Sannyasa* (period of dissemination of spiritual knowledge). Similarly four sections of the community are constituted according to their inherent nature and qualities, otherwise everyone is equal. It is our qualities and actions which make differentiation and not birth. Although these classifications are not fast and rigid and are not observed in modern times, yet they are on the whole the main natural divisions of life and sections of the community at large. All castes (sections) are important like the limbs of the body. No section of the community should be looked down upon. All sects are equally important.

Without performing obligatory duties none can attain the stage of non-desire. It is a fallacy to think of reaching this stage by neglecting one's obligations. To reach the upper storey of a house a staircase is needed. A boat should not be discarded when one has yet to cross a river. So long as there is no freedom from desire, there is action. Desire is the cause of bondage. It arises from mind and has no limitations. By the rise of contentment, desire spontaneously disappears. One should not turn away from one's duties if one aims at the final liberation. It is not possible for one to perform actions or to abandon them at will. To talk of relinquishing actions is to talk of impossibility, because, however one may wish, one cannot abandon them. Further, one sets an example for others by performing one's duties. Even those who have attained self-realization have to continue to do actions as long as they have body for the sake of humanity at large. In this way the wise guide others and persuade the ignorant to perform the right type of action. If you really want to attain constant peace, perform all your actions with your heart devoted to the self, and offer them unto God. Never think 'this is action and I am doing it with a particular object.' A man who does not attach himself to the fruit of action, while doing everything, is not affected.

If actions are done as a Yajna, sacrifice, at the altar of divine will, they are spiritualised and liberate the doer instead of causing bondage, reaction and rebirth.

> Thy business is with the action only, never with its fruit. Be not instrument in making your action bear fruit, nor let your attachment be in action.
>
> *Bhagavad Gita,* II.47

> He who totally gives up attachment to actions and their fruits, has got over the dependence on the world, and is ever satisfied, does nothing at all, though he may be ever engaged in action.
>
> *Bhagavad Gita,* IV.20

> He who acts, offering all actions to God, and shaking off attachment remains untouched by sin, as a lotus leaf is untouched by water.
>
> *Bhagavad Gita,* V.10

> Offering fruit of action to God, the Karma Yogi attains peace in the shape of God-realization, whereas he who works with selfish motives being attached to the fruit of action through desires, gets tied down.
>
> *Bhagavad Gita,* V.12

"What shall I do to inherit eternal life?" was the question put to Christ and his answer was, "Do thy duty for duty's sake."

"Work is worship and man's homage to the Supreme", Lord says in Bhagavad Gita:

> He from whom all beings arise and by whom all this is pervaded by worshipping him, through the performance of his own duty does man attain perfection.
>
> (XVIII.46)

Emerson sings :

> *Teach me your mood, O patient stars,*
> *who climb each night to ancient sky,*
> *Leaving no space, no shade, no scars,*
> *No trace of age, no fear to die.*

Did the sun, the moon, the stars ever demand wages for their so punctual and regular service? Did the trees ever use their own fruits, enjoy their own shades? Did the flowers ever smell their own fragrance or enjoy their own beauty? Why should a man expect fruits of action, which he is incapable of doing without the support of the Overself? The result of any action depends upon several other factors beyond one's control, like the ripening of harvest which requires timely rains, timely sunshine and natural safety besides the labour, protection and care of the cultivator.

A wise man should be careful and vigilant not to be slave of senses. Remember that the desire associated with sense creates a mirage of happiness which fades away as you go nearer. You must, therefore, ruthlessly avoid prohibited actions and never desire the undesirable. All actions arise through the functions of the senses and thus discipline of the senses is needed. Brihadaranyaka Upanishad says, "Desire makes the man. His action follows his desire and so his attainment follows his action." Thus individual karmas are created. There is an English proverb, "Sow a thought, reap a habit; sow a habit, reap a character; sow a character, reap a destiny."

The best way to control desire or anger is to trace its source, to control the senses first and that will make the mind steady and peaceful. An uncontrolled mind is the root of all troubles. A man who remains even-minded, steady and cheerful amid all distractions can only remain happy.

The fruits of actions have got to be borne by those who do not abandon the desire for the fruits. A man who has become the father of a daughter, owes his duties to the daughter as long as he does not say that she is not his and performs the ceremony of her gift in marriage.

Then his son-in-law becomes responsible for his daughter as wife. It is only when one neglects one's duties and is inclined to erroneous acts that one is caught in the cycle of life and death. The performance of one's duty for duty's sake is in itself the highest sacrifice (yajna), and a man who is devoted to such sacrifice is free from all bonds.

Karma Yoga is the performance of Karmas. Buddhi Yoga (Jnana Yoga) is not possible by abandoning actions. You must realize that the only thing which is worth doing is one's duty without attachment to the result. Do nothing which is prohibited and always pursue that which is right without any selfish motive and without any desire. Zealously devote yourself to right actions and perform them with diligence and without expectations. Do not be puffed up if you succeed or be disheartened if the action remains unsuccessful, because the merit of it is not lost. Whatever you do, should be dedicated to the Lord of Creation and that is in itself the completion of action. One can be free from the cycle of birth and death and enjoy the true happiness of life if one can remain indifferent to the results while performing action.

> He must not desire any fruit or reward of his actions.
>
> *Adi Granth Sahib*

Rabindranath Tagore says:

> In my work is my joy and in the joy does the joy of joy abide.

> Success in every undertaking depends on destiny and man combined. The acts of destiny are out of control of man. Think not of destiny, but act yourself.
>
> *Manu Smriti,* VII.205

> Penance, study and surrendering fruits of action to God are called Kriya Yoga (Karma Yoga).
>
> *Yoga Sutra,* II.1

He who is steadfast in his heart, absorbed in the self, outwardly pursues the normal worldly activities of life, he who is not afraid of objects of senses, who does not neglect to perform obligatory actions, such a person (*Yogi*) is worthy of reverence and respect. A sage living in the world appears like everybody else, just as the orb of the sun reflected in water appears like the sun, but the sun is not there in reality. Therefore, the Lord emphasizes the necessity of controlling the mind. Be firm and pure in your heart and let the senses perform their actions freely. Do everything which is opportune and proper. Whosoever performs actions arising as a result of duties, in his own conditions of life, he certainly attains liberation as a natural consequence. A fish perishes when out of water, so does a man who forgets his duties.

> A man who employs all his available resources for performing proper action without any desire for fruits, who offers the worship ordained and who discharges his obligation to his ancestors, who enjoys what remains to himself, after he has done this with his family, he is free from all evils. His sins disappear like the night at the break of the day.

The essence of the law of action is that the actions are spiritualised and energised by the love of humanity and by using our intelligence and will for the good of all living beings, and shedding the narrow and selfish motive or desire for fruits.

Milton sang:

> People think that happiness lies in being served by others, while it really lies in serving others.

> 'Whosoever doth service without any desire, findeth God'.

Adi Granth

> With self-control and having equal regard for all, they, too, who are attached to the service of all beings, attain me.

Bhagavad Gita, XII.4

In every stage of life, in whatever sphere we may be, we will find opportunity to help and assist others and we must keep this in mind while discharging our duties in office, factory, shop or business house. This attitude of helping others automatically prevents a person from being unjust and dishonest. A shopkeeper will not adulterate foodstuff or manipulate the prices, a politician will forgo his personal interest, position and prestige for the sake of national interest, a government servant will live on his real income and thus, each one will be following Karma Yoga in practice. We forget that what we sow now, we will have to reap. Nature is not in a hurry to settle the accounts. She is not partial to any; she waits for the right moment and, sooner or later, we will have to pay for our misdeeds. It is the immutable Law of Nature, the Law of Cause and Effect. It is, therefore, in our own interest not to start a cause by dishonest or illegitimate means. Nature's mill grinds slowly but surely.

I visited European countries. I stayed in U.S.A. and U.K. I find, citizens there observe the laws of their country. They are generally honest in their day-to-day living. Traffic on the roads is disciplined without a policeman. Departmental stores show courtesy and consideration to the customers. They accept and refund the money paid for the articles not approved, even after a week or so without demur. Foodstuffs are never adulterated. (But a recent study in India indicated that consumers are cheated to the tune of Rs. 20,000 millions a year.) Drugs and medicines are not spurious or sold without the physician's prescription. Government offices have a helpful attitude towards the public and there is no corruption or harassment. Things go by rules and regulations. Average citizens are not bothered or put to inconvenience or delays. Let us in India follow their good example in our daily living.

Man is a social being. He has to live in society. In the good of others lies his own good. The expectation and thinking about the fruit of actions will cause pain and sorrow. So it is better to avoid them.

I will close this chapter with a prayer from Gurudev Rabindranath Tagore:

This is the prayer to Thee my Lord—

> *Strike strike at the root of penury in my heart.*
> *Give me the strength to bear my joys and sorrows.*
> *Give me the strength to make my love fruitful in service.*
> *Give me the strength never to disown the poor or bend my knees before insolent might.*
> *Give me the strength to raise my mind high above daily trifles.*

5

BHAKTI YOGA

Bhakti is a general term, covering several methods of worship. It generally means one's devotedness to some deity of one's choice (*sagun upasana*) and adoring Him with great devotion and love by outward rituals. As people are lost in the names and forms in this world, idol worship and rituals are suggested to divert their minds towards God (Who is given name and form). He is symbolically represented in the idol for easy concentration as abstract concentation (worship of *Nirguna Brahma*) is not possible for all seekers.* Different deities are various cosmic forces, emanating from one source, and working in this universe. It is like a single electric current which can perform hundreds of functions, light bulbs, run fans, machines and many other instruments.

Sri Shankaracharya defines Bhakti as devotion unto Atman. It is a path of trust and love. It is surrender to Divine Will. A devotee shows intense faith and love for God.

Bhakti has generally been classified as under:

1. (a) Apara (lower) — It means observing rituals and ceremonies prescribed by particular sect or religion, for example, a Hindu worshipper goes to temple, applies sandalpaste, burns incense, rings bell and performs other rituals in routine.

   (b) Para (higher) — Signifies a worshipper free from three gunas (sattva, rajas, tamas) and any motive or desire. Such a devotee has universal love. He wishes good of all. It is the highest culminating point in devotion. Ram Dev, Tukaram, Tulsidas, and Hafiz followed this type of Bhakti.

---

* See *Bhagavadgita,* XII.5.

2. (a) Ragatmika — (primary or mukhya)-It is a free flow of Divine without any binding or limitation. The devotee is like an innocent and simple child and pours his love for the Beloved, like Meera and Gopis of Vrindavan.
   (b) Vidhi — Devotee observes rules and ceremonies.

3. (a) Sakama is Gauna or secondary type of devotion with motive and desire for wealth, worldly comforts and children.
   (b) Nishkama — Devotion without any desire for fruit.

4. (a) Vyabhicharini — To love God with some purpose such as to possess a wife, sons and property.
   (b) Avyabhicharini—To love God alone for ever and ever.

There is hardly any difference between Para Bhakti, Ananya Bhakti and Avyabhicharini Bhakti.

Bhakti is governed by three qualities, namely,

(a) Sattvika — to please God and to destroy one's attachment to senses.
(b) Rajasika — to get wealth, fame and property.
(c) Tamasika— to worship for the destruction of enemy and to get success even through unlawful means.

In the Bhagavad Gita the Lord says:

'Four types of men worship Me, Arjuna, a seeker of worldly objects, a sufferer, a seeker of knowledge, and a man of wisdom."

VII.16

"Of these, the best is the man of wisdom, ever established in identity with Me and possessed of exclusive devotion. For I am extremely dear to the wise (who knows Me in reality) and he is extremely dear to Me."

VII-17

There are five kinds of emotions *(bhava)* in Bhakti:

1. Shanta Bhava (peaceful emotion).
2. Dasya Bhava (considering oneself as a slave/servant of God).
3. Vatsalya Bhava (considering God as a Father-Mother).
4. Sakhya Bhava (considering God as a friend like Arjuna and Krishna).

5. Madhurya Bhava is a most difficult mode of Vedanta Sadhana. It is merging in Him.

One emotion (Bhava) embraces the other.

A devotee starts from fine emotion, which develops into warm affection and then in glowing love and ultimately into the supreme and unbounded love. When a devotee advances in devotion to the Lord, he sheds tears of delight. He may cry or laugh. He may sing or dance in Divine Ecstasy.

When devotion matures, it brings jnana (wisdom) to the devotee. Bhakta is also a jnani. It is only at the time of intense devotion and love that mind becomes void and free.

In the scriptures, the following stages of Bhakti are mentioned:

1. Satsang (good company of saints).
2. Svadhyaya (study of holy scriptures).
3. Stuti (admiration).
4. Shraddha (faith in God).
5. Bhakti (devotion to God).
6. Nishtha (devotedness).
7. Ruchi (hearing and chanting His name).
8. Rati (intense attachment to Lord).
9. Sthayi Bhava (steadiness).
10. Prema-maya (the devotee at this stage has no attachment to worldly objects and lives and moves in Divine ecstasy).

Briefly there are nine modes of Bhakti:

1. Shravana (hearing of Divine glory).
2. Kirtana (singing praises of Him with Bhava [emotion] and devotion).
3. Smarana (remembering His name).
4. Padasevana (service and presence at the feet of the Lord).
5. Archana (worship).
6. Vandana (prostration to God).
7. Dasya (cultivating Bhava of a servant).
8. Sakhya (cultivating Bhava of a friend).
9. Atma-Nivedana (complete self-surrender).

There are 16 limbs of Puja (ritual worship) of a Deity:

1. Asana: offering seat for the Deity.

2. Svagata: welcome the Deity with prayer (mantra).
3. Padya: washing the feet.
4. Arghya: water offering made in a vessel.
5. Achamana: sipping of water.
6. Madhuparka: honey, ghee, milk and curd
7. Snana: bathing.
8. Vastra: garment.
9. Bhushana: ornaments and jewels.
10. Gandha: perfume.
11. Pushpa: flowers.
12. Dhoopa: incense.
13. Dipa: light.
14. Naivedya: food offering.
15. Tambula: betel leaf.
16. Vandana or Namaskara: prostration and prayer.

The accessories of worship mentioned above have inner meanings as mentioned below:*

Arghya	(water) used in worship is a symbol of pervasiveness and an object for purification.
Bhushana	(ornaments) placed on image symbolise the virtues of the Deity who is immortal.
Gandha	(perfume) stands for the perception of consciousness pervading the earth of which the physical body is made. Sense of smell is connected with the Prithvi Tattva (earth).
Pushpa	(flowers) offering of flowers indicates perception of consciousness pervading the Akasha Tattva (ether).
Dhoopa	(incense) stands for perception of consciousness pervading the Vayu Tattva (air).
Dipa	(light) stands for perception of consciousness pervading the Agni Tattva (fire).
Yajna	(fire) stands for transmutation. Agni is a great transformer in nature.
Arati	(waving of lights) stands for discarding of the object of thought which is the inanimate world.
Naivedya	(food)Food sustains life. Offering of food stands for the perception of the principle of immortality. Rice as food stands for the perception of Existence- Consciousness-Experience in all things.

* Karapatri, "Shri Bhagavati Tattva" *Siddhanta* V.

Vandana (obeisance and praise) Obeisance stands for dissolution of all thoughts into the Principle-of-All. Prayer and praise offerings stand for the dissolution of words into the word principle.

A sadhak has to lead a life as a ritual, a life in harmony with universal pattern. The whole of human existence is considered as participation in cosmic symphony.

The ancient seers and sages have embodied the secrets of worship in daily rituals to keep the ideas alive generation after generation.

Give me the boon of devotion (Bhakti)
O my Guru, God of Gods,
nothing more I desire
save Thy service day and night.

Kabir Sahib

As snake is charmed by sweet melodious sound,
so also the snake-mind is charmed by
melodious dhvani of sankirtan

Swami Sivananda

It's the flame of Love that fired me,
It's the wine of Love which inspired me,
Woulds't Thou learn how lovers bleed,
Hearken, hearken to the reed.

Maulana Rumi

There are eight signs of progress in the Path of Devotion :

(1) Tears, (2) horripilation, (3) tremor, (4) weeping, (5) laughing, (6) perspiration, (7) fainting, and (8) inability to speak.

Sri Ramanuja has mentioned eleven points for developing and intensifying Bhakti:

1. Abhyasa—Practice—to be regular and punctual in daily sadhana.
2. Viveka—Discrimination—to know what is right and what is wrong.
3. Satya—Truth—to be true in words and deeds.
4. Arjava—Straightforwardness, avoid cunningness.
5. Kriya—Doing good to others—i.e. rendering selfless service
6. Kalyana—Wishing good of all, i.e. never to harm anyone by thought, word or deed.
7. Daya—Compassion—to be merciful and to forgive others' fault.

8. Ahimsa—Non-injury.
9. Dana—Charity.
10. Anavasada—Freedom from sorrow—to remain balanced in calamity.
11. Prasanta—Cheerfulness—try to be cheerful in all conditions.

Bhakti is love, devotion and faith. Love is the highest kind of beauty. Love generates love. In Bhakti one should be simple like a child, loving like a lover.

> Verily I say unto you, except ye turn and become as little children, ye shall not enter into the kingdom of heaven.
>
> *Christ*

> Yoga cannot equal love, nor can Jnana; without love and devotion, O mystics, all contemplation is void.
>
> *Kabir Sahib*

> The same am I to all beings; there is none hateful to me nor dear. They verily who worship Me, with devotion, are in Me and I also in them.
>
> *Bhagavad Gita* IX.29

6

JAPA YOGA

Let me be Thine, O Love!
But for an hour;
I yield my heart and soul
Unto Thy power;
Let me be Thine,
O, Love of mine,
But for an hour.

Japa is an oral or mental repetition of a sacred divine name, with intense devotion, love and without motive or expectation of fruit. It is an inner outburst of pure love for the Supreme.

A Muslim also repeats Kalmah (mantra) of the Quran, so deeply absorbed that his whole body may ring with the mystic sound. They call it Shugal-i-issme-zat or Zikar-i-famida.

In the beginning Japa is performed from the tip of the tongue loudly. Then the mantra is repeated mentally from the centre of the throat. Then the mantra descends deeper into the centre of the heart. Further, it goes deeper into the naval centre. Step by step the chanter progresses on the path of Japa Yoga, as he goes from Vaikhari (loudly) to Madhyama (whispering) and then to Para and Pashyanti (mental japa) from the heart or navel centre. The deeper the japa goes, the more powerful it becomes. When the mantra is repeated mentally and seems to be vibrating from inside, you are nearing the destination. Mantra should be taken from a Guru (a mantra-seer).

Performance of nama-japa with love, devotion can mitigate the ill-effect of Planets in a person's horoscope at the time of birth as well as the periodical (Dasa) effects of the stars.

Potency and meaning of the mantra should be understood. The chanter should not think himself different from the mantra. Japa and the Deity, whose mantra is recited, are identical. Lord Shiva said to Parvati:

मन्त्रो मद्रूपः वरानने

O, Beauteous one, Mantra is My very Form.

The world is the creation of sound;sound has vibrations. In mantras sounds are combined to give certain powerful vibrations which unfold and expand the human consciousness. Actually this whole universe is a play of different vibrations and energies working at different levels. Behind every living being, there is a specific vibration which keeps together the different components as an organic whole and the moment that vibration ceases, the form disintegrates.

A lonely, clean and airy place in the house should be set apart for japa. This should exclusively be used for mantra japa, meditation, study of scriptures and for no other purpose, and may preferably be kept under lock and key, if possible.

If you can afford to get a suitable place outside your house on the bank of a river or under a tree in a garden, so much the better. Here you should make your seat of kusa grass, deer/tiger skin or woollen blanket covered with white cotton cloth. It should be little raised from the ground. The time of japa is just after getting up from the bed or just before going to bed or when it is *Sandhyakala* (junction time), a time when mind is naturally in a relaxed state. Early morning from 3 a. m. to sunrise is *Brahma muhurta* (moments of the divine), as the world is still asleep and there is peculiar calmness prevailing in the atmosphere. At this time there is a pale bluish light coming from the East, containing subtle force of magnetism or vital energy which affects the brain.

These light rays give lustre and energy to the body and stimulate the brain cells. After sunrise various forces begin to work and natural calmness of the atmosphere is disturbed. The sunrise, sunset, midday, midnight are also *sandhyakalas*, when Nature has a special effect on concentration of mind.

Ekadasi (11th Moon), *Amavasya* (no-Moon) and *Purnima* (full Moon) are particular days for the practice of intensive meditation, as on these days the Moon exercises a tremendous influence on the ocean waves, as well as on the human mind, and the spiritual forces are released by the Providence for the aid of the seekers.

Seated firmly in an easy posture, like *padma, siddha,* or *svastika asana,* with head, neck and back straight and eyes and ears * closed, one should perform japa. In this posture you can concentrate on your beloved Lord (Deity) and His divine virtues, repeating his name with profound reverence, devotion and love, also listening to it attentively and understanding its meanings. Mantra is power in the form of sound. It comes from the root '*man*' meaning 'to think'.

You should sit as long as you can concentrate. Then you gradually prolong this period. Slowly the substance of mind will take the shape of the 'syllable mantra' repeated. The mind will be purified and the worshipper will melt into the object of worship and the seer, the sadhana and the sight will become one.

While practising japa, the devotee's mind, sometimes, and quite unknowingly, gets externalised or diffused, but at other times, it reaches a great depth of profound concentration. The difficulty is that the change or transition from concentrated to the diffused state of mind and vice versa is beyond the detection of the devotee himself. He should, therefore, remain awake, aware and watchful.

Further, you should be very vigilant and careful to avoid drowsiness and sleepiness and to ensure that utterance of holy name, syllable, does not become a routine work. You should start japa immediately after the supervention of sleep ceases and must not bemoan such supervention, as it happens in the early stages in most of the cases, and there will be no use of such regret. When such interruption seems imminent, you may adopt the posture known as *'vajra asana'*(sitting on knees) and start pranayama (deep breathing) or japa or repeat the name of Lord loudly or sing His glories.

I reiterate with great emphasis that the repetition of divine name should be of the nature of religious emotion and the mind itself must function as speech, while the organ of speech is still and at perfect rest, whereby the mind remains perspicacious of the articulation of mantra. In this condition the movement of the mind is easily perceptible. You should watch the intrusion of extraneous thought as and when it occurs. It is a state of mind when perception transcends the limitation of senses. The success will not dawn until you disband conflicting thoughts and desires and come at peace with yourself and reach the gate of silence.

> When in remembering God, dost thou loseth thyself, thou findest the way to His Darbar.

• Ears may be closed with cotton or rubber plugs as outside noise generally causesdistraction.

Bu Ali

Repeat holy name and by repetition do thou attain happiness and remove pain and troubles from the body.

Adi Granth Sahib

By repetition of mantras, comes realization of the intended Deity.

Yoga Sutra, II.44

When clothes are dirty, they are washed with soap; when mind gets polluted with sin, by God 's name it is washed.

Sri Guru Nanak Dev

Of all the yajnas, I am the jap yajna.

Bhagavad Gita

मधुरं मधुरेभ्योऽपि मङ्गलेभ्योऽपि मङ्गलम्
पावनं पावनेभ्योऽपि हरेर्नामैव केवलम् ॥

If there is anything sweeter than all sweet things, more auspicious than all auspicious objects, and more purifying than all purifying agencies, it is the name of Hari and Hari alone.

नामा म्हणे नाम, चैतन्य निज धाम

The name of God is the very abode of consciousness.

Sri Namdev

Japa is the most effective way of achieving the fourfold aim of life. It can be practised with ease and yields great result with least effort.

Sri Shankaracharya

Every atom of your body should be throbbing, thrilling or vibrating with remembrance of God. *Ramanama* is a pill of *Ananda* (Bliss); when taken, it enters and pervades the whole body.

Swami Ramdas

7

DHYANA YOGA

The japa is followed by visualizing in the mind the Ishta Devata (the personal Deity) whose mantra is repeated by the aspirant with con-centration. For each mantra there is a particular form of Ishta Devata (Deity) prescribed in our shastras. Before contemplating on Divine form of Deity, a beginning is made with the following practices:

1. Look at a black dot on a white paper or cloth in front of you at a distance of about two feet without winking your eyes, as long as you can.
2. Place a good mirror before you and stare into your eyes without blinking for about 30 minutes daily. You have to start with two minutes and increase the period gradually and comfortably. The room should be dark. A candle flame may be kept beside the mirror. After three weeks or so you may not see your face! Now close your eyes and encounter with your own sub-conscious mind. A mirror should be used specifically for this purpose and should be kept wrapped in crimson-coloured cloth after use.
3. A yogi may fix his gaze at the space which appears diversified with the rays of sun, moon, or lamp. He will realize his real nature.

   Verse 76, *Vijnana Bhairava Tantra*

4. A yogi may sit at ease placing his arms like a bow overhead, and fix his gaze at his armpits. He will experience peace and tranquility.

   Verse 79, *Vijnana Bhairava Tantra*

5. Visualise in your mind a beautiful garden or a beautiful flower or a beautiful scenery which is most alluring and charming and appealing to you.
6. You should first picture in imagination a particular form of the

Formless, which you love most and dwell on that allowing your feelings to flow out towards That in affection, adoration and admiration. You should vísualise yourself in His benign presence. If you are lucky and perseverant, you may one day actualise your visualization. There are persons who are blessed with Divine Vision. I have met them.

Gradually you will begin to realize with ardent devotion the fine characteristics of the Divine nature and will ultimately perceive it in all things and everywhere. Concentration of any form leads to the vision of the Principle beyond that form. Concentration is easier on a form or idol than on invisible and abstract Immense Being. By practice you will begin to feel that all exists in Him and He permeates everything. This will be the day of explosion, which will take you to the abode of bliss, purity, silence and innocence. You will enjoy the ecstasy and drink the nectar that flows in such lively moments :

Thou will keep him in perfect peace,
Whose mind (thoughts and imagination)
is stayed on Thee.

Images are symbolic. They represent divine forces working and controlling the universe. These forces (Gods) are present in the universe, in atoms, in human beings and everywhere and in everything, as living principle or as presiding consciousness, which is not directly perceptible to our sense.

Idol is in the likeness of the Original. It is symbolic interpretation of what has been seen in trance (samadhi) by the ancient sages.

The idea behind the cult of images is to worship the invisible through the visible.

Karapatri, Lingopasana Rahasya Siddhanta

Because the unrealised have not the capacity of worshipping divinity in its true form, they should accept the help of images.

Tantra-Sara Sangraha

But those who depending exclusively on Me, and surrendering all actions to Me (God with attributes) constantly meditate on Me, with single-minded devotion, I speedily deliver them from the ocean of birth and death.

Bhagavad Gita, XII.6, 7

8

AJAPAJAPA YOGA

You can mentally repeat 'so' (सो) while inhaling the breath and 'ham' (हं) with the exhalation of breath or vice versa. While doing so, it is necessary that the eyes should be directed towards the tip of nose, or toward *trikuti* (place between two eyebrows). This centre is also referred to as the *Ajna Chakra* or the third eye and the Muslim mystics speak of it as *nuktt-e-sawaida'*. Ajapajapa is called *pas-anfas'* by Muslim mystics.

The sound of 'so ham' is produced while breathing in and out in a natural way. *'So 'ham'* means 'What thou art, the same am I'. Muslim mystics speak of it as a *'an-a-hu'* and Mansur uttered this reality as the *'anl-ḥaq'*, that is, 'I am reality'.

After some time it may be started by exhaling, and repeating mentally *'Ham'* and *'so'* when inhaling. It turns out as *'ham'* and *'so'*. While meditating, ensure that you are seated comfortably in an easy posture, and be conscious of the fact that you are breathing and feel the ingoing breath as it reaches the navel. Also be conscious of breath when it comes out from the navel. After doing japa, pause without thinking of anything, be void and empty of thoughts and stay in this state for a few moments. As a diver dives deep into the ocean to pick up some pearls from the bottom, similarly dive deep into the ocean of bliss, and thereby, by losing yourself, enjoy the blissful moments of divine embrace.

You can also separate 'so' and 'ham' while exhaling and inhaling while leaving some gap (space) between the two.

> Hamsa automatically becomes 'so ham' by repetition
>
> The 'So' ham' ajapajapa destroys all sins and virtues.
>
> *Kabir*

> As you become aware of Soham, the body consciousness dissolves and the senses, which have been wandering among outer objects, automatically turn within.
>
> — *Sant Jnaneshvar*

In japa yoga, 'Aum' is the most important, original and unconditional sound principle. Gopinath Kaviraj says that some ancient cults of yoga have explained it by the term 'sphota', the meaning of which is to 'burst and split'. It is the corresponding word for Brahman (the Eternal Being).

It is a sign, a symbol, a secret key. It is the deepest sound of cosmic music, uncreated, "anahata", universal sound, sound of existence. All mantras are to be preceded by this key word and end with it. It signifies the ultimate reality as the creator, the sustainer and the finality. Through this "word of prayer" the supreme is invoked and adored excellently.

> He is known as *AUM*. *Yoga Sutra,* I.27
>
> Repeating and meditating on AUM brings about the disappearance of all obstacles and an awakening of a new consciousness.
>
> *Yoga Sutra,* I.29

After three gross steps, A, U and M, there are two subtle steps, the end of which sound as mmm and then comes soundlessness. It implies five bodies (sheaths) of human being and five states of mind. 'Amen' of Mohammedans and the word 'Omni' (in Latin language), i.e. omniscient, omnipotent, resembles AUM, and may have originated from it. As Sanskrit word Dhyana (meditation) became 'Jhana' in Buddhist Pali language and then became 'Ch'an in China (where it was carried by a famous Buddhist missionary, Bodhidharma). Later it became 'Zen' in Japan. It is the Japanese way of writing and speaking of 'Ch'an'. So, AUM can change to 'Amen' or 'Omni', or ON in Egypt; as Risi (meaning venerable spiritual teacher) can change to Roshis in Japan and Shiva can became Zev, Jov. Linguists say that words and their pronunciations change, when they travel to other countries and climates.

Aum is the symbol of union of three gods. It is the most abstract symbol of divinity and the instrument of realization. Aum, the total vovel sound, reverberates in the universe and in the cavern of heart, when all outer sound has ceased.

Aum. This syllable is the whole world. It is the past, the present, the future. Everything is just the word AUM. And whatever else there is that transcends threefold time, that, too, is just one word Aum.

Mandukya Upanisad, 1.1

This one syllable 'Aum' is formed of eight subtle sound elements. It has an eightfold character, is divisible into eight parts. A is the first, U, the second, M, the third. The nasalization (bindu) is the fourth; the sound (nada) is the fifth; the duration (kala) is the sixth; the resonance within time (kalatita) is the seventh. In addition to these its timeless resonance is the eighth.

Tarasara Upanisad, 2.1

One should concentrate one's mind on OM, (for) OM is Brahman beyond fear. For man ever fixed in Brahman can have no fear anywhere.

ibid, 1.25

O, Parvati, by repeating 'Aum' methodically and concentrating in the mind on the void at the end of the protracted phase of it, the Yogi attains oneness with Divine.

Vijnana Bhairava Tantra, Verse, 39

Aum is indisputably acceptable to all,
Short name of the Immutable as the Vedas call,
Redeems the soul from the physical bondage,
Makes it realise its immortal heritage.

ओमित्येकाक्षरं ब्रह्म व्याहरन्मामनुस्मरन् ।
यः प्रयाति त्यजन्देहं स याति परमां गतिम् ॥

Aum is the one indestructible (sound),
the Immensity. He who leaves this world,
uttering this syllable Aum, with his mind
intent on Me, attains to the Supreme Goal.

Bhagavad Gita, VIII.13

ॐ इत्येकाक्षरं ब्रह्म। ॐ जगत्। ॐ सर्वम्।

Aum is one word Brahman
Aum is universe,
Aum is All.
Brahman is in the form of one syllable, Aum

Aum is the universe, Aum is all.
When Aum rises, the Universe rises.
Aum is the creative symbol of all
elements of principles.

Siddha Meditation

The sound of Aum should be created through mind. In the beginning it can be chanted loudly, prolonged as far as one can breathe (*Om Dhvani*). (See illustration). You should hear it when you pronounce it. You should stop and let the sound echo itself. It should come in a natural, spontaneous and simple way. Let it saturate your body and mind.

While repeating, meditate on it and remain aware, and when you advance in japa you are completely lost and there is pure consciousness, a flame of light and chanting is all round. This happened to Swami Ramtirtha when he was sleeping in his hut in a forest (Himalayas). His companion, Sardar Puransingh, heard the chanting of "Ram-Ram" loudly. He went out for the person who was chanting. He could not find anyone. The place was lonely and solitary. When he came back and was nearer to Swami Ram Tirtha, who was fast asleep, he found that the sound was coming from his sleeping body, which was vibrating with the sound Ram -Ram, like the vibrations we feel from the loud speaker of a T.V. or radio by putting our ears or fingers near it.

Patanjali says:

The repetition of this 'Aum' and meditating on its meanings (is the way).

Yoga Sutra, I.28

Besides Aum and Ardha mantra, there are four other parts of Aum viz ; Bindu (Dot), Bija (Seed), Shakti (Power) and Shanti (Peace). These are to be felt through intense feelings (Bhavana) during meditation on "AUM". Aum contains all the seven vibrations as sunlight contains seven colours.

A represents vishva getting dissolved in Virat.
U is tejas which gets dissolved in Hiranyagarbha (Cosmic egg).
M prajna gets merged in Ishvara (God).

Omkara created God 'Brahma'

Aum Mandala—Vibrations spreading from Aum Dhvani

Omkara does He adore.
Omkara created Yugas (The cycles of Time)
Omkara revealed the Vedas

Guru Nanak Sahib

In Gayatri Mantra, 'Savitr' is the Lord of creation, whose glorious symbol in the universe is the solar orb. Gayatri mantra is the mantra of the Vedas. It is found in all the four Vedas, without any change. Gayatri is said to be the same as Parvati, the celestial spouse of Lord Siva.

Sir John Woodroffe writes:

"A mantra is composed of certain letters arranged in definite sequence of sounds of which the letters are the representative signs. To produce the desired effect of the mantra, it must be intoned in a proper way according to rhythm (Svara) and Varna (Sound). So mantra when translated loses its sound effect and becomes a mere sentence.

Jean Le Mee writes:

"Mantar (man-tra) min-d-ins-tru-ment, whose rules are rules of thought, is said to have the ability to re-create in the prepared hearer, the experience of the poet, the rishi."

Kabir Says:

Ram practices my japa, while I sit relaxed.

हमारा जप करे राम, हम बैठे आराम

9

SAMARPANA (SELF-SURRENDER)

Success is also attained by those who surrender to God.

Yoga Sutra, I.23

Hear thou again my Supreme Word, most secret of all; because thou art dearly beloved of Me, therefore, I will tell thee what is good.

Bhagavad Gita, XVIII.64

Fix thy mind on Me, be devoted to
Me, sacrifice to Me, bow down to Me;
So shalt thou come to me.
Truly do I promise into thee
(for) thou art dear to Me

Bhagavad Gita, XVIII.63

Abandoning all duties, take refuge
in Me alone; I will liberate thee from all sins,
grieve not.

Bhagavad Gita, XVII.66

It is interesting to mention here that the word Islam is derived from an Arabic verb signifying the idea of submission to the Supreme Will.

Submission or surrender to the higher Will in terms of all that one is and has, is the only proper course for the human soul to take. Do your work as an offering unto God. Work is worship if done in the right spirit. Surrender your mind, feelings, intellect and everything unto the lotus-feet of the Lord.

Take refuge in the Divine will. The infinite world is being controlled and directed by the Supreme Intelligence. It is moving and working under certain laws, and so merge your little self into the Supreme and break your limitations. Radha asked Lord Krishna why He loved His flute so much ? The Lord replied that the flute had done great penance (tapasya) for him. For years it tolerated the hot sun and heavy rains and then got itself cut. Holes were bored into its body. It got itself emptied so that He can play upon it. So it was dear to Him.

In actual life, you are always pre-occupied and filled with thought, emotions and desires that there is no room for the Divine to enter or manifest.

Make room for the Divine to manifest itself in you. No sooner do you surrender yourself entirely, without reservations, then you are surely to find Him waiting for you in the innermost chambers of your heart.

O Lord, my God, do Thou thy holy Will,
I will lie still
I will not stir, lest I forsake Thine arm
and break the charm,
Which lulls me clinging to my
Father's breast in perfect rest.

Renunciation is not to be so much of the body as of the mind. You need not renounce the world, which is a great school for training your will, testing your character and developing your talents and energies. If, while remaining in the world, you remain away from its temptations you are really a brave man and will lead a divine life, which is expected to be led by a man who is the crown of God's creation.

You can make everything Divine through surrender as it invokes Divinity. If you resolve to live and grow with the great law of self-surrender to the Divine Will, you will feel free, without worry or mental tension. Do not keep your luggage on your lap or on your head while travelling in a train. The train will carry you as well as your luggage.

While marching on the path of surrender, some day "something" can happen to you in a natural way, as 'happening' is the phenomenon on the path of surrender. Whatever is done is done with Him, through Him, by Him, to Him.

O Love, I give myself to Thee,
Thine ever, only Thine to be.
Commit to Him thine every way,
And He will keep thee day by day
Thy righteousness shines as the light.
Thy judgment as the noonday bright.

Charles F. Sheldon, D.D.

In Sufism "Baqa" is to awaken and to absorb the Divine consciousness by surrendering oneself completely to Allah and is considered the highest achievement.

Calling out for Thee, I became even Thyself
and in me is left no 'I' O, to Thy name do
I sacrifice myself for whichever way the
eye looketh, Thee is beholdeth.

Maulana Rumi

So long as he loses not himself,
no man findeth the way to the
Darbar of Almighty.

Maulana Rumi

When thou thyself shall cease to be,
then the beloved Lord would thou find
therefore, O thou wise man, try to lose thyself.

Maulana Rumi

Humble and mute acceptance of Divine Authority
makes life 's journey easier.

Mahatma Gandhi

Let Love 's bright sunshine play upon your heart.
Come now unto your gladness, peace and rest
Bid the dark shades of selfishness depart,
And now and evermore be truly blest.
Too narrow is the lane of love for
Two to be together, when I was, God
was not, now He is, I am not.

Kabir

We are mere instruments in His Divine hands Let Him wield as He wills. Our surrender to His Will brings us immediate freedom, peace and bliss.

Swami Ramdas

10

PURNA YOGA

Purna Yoga is similar to self-surrender as mentioned earlier.

It is to leave oneself entirely at the mercy of the Divine power to allow It to mould oneself (devotee) as It wills. The devotee becomes like a clay, wax, plaster of Paris in the hands of the Divine artist, or like a musical instrument in the hands of a great musician or like a floor under the feet of the Cosmic Dancer (*Nataraja*).

When Nature wants to drill a man,
and thrill a man
and skill a man
When Nature wants to mould a man
To play the noblest part,
When She yearns with all Her heart
To create so great and bold a man
That all the world shall praise —
Watch Her method and watch Her ways!
How She ruthlessly perfects
Whom She royally elects ;
How She hammers him and hurts him,
And with mighty blows converts him
Into trial shapes of clay which only Nature
Understands—
While his tortured heart is crying and He
lifts beseeching hands;
When She bends but never breaks,
When his good She undertakes.
How She uses whom She chooses
And with every purpose infuses him,
By every art induces him
To try his splendour out;

Nature knows what She's about.

Angela Morgan

A purna yogi tries to mould his life according to the inner divinity. He is patient, perseverant, has perfect control over his body and mind. He follows his path of complete self-annihilation and openness to the Divine Will. He keeps his courage in the face of difficulty, and when a storm of difficulties comes in the sea of his life, he does not lose courage. He braves the storm and high waves and keeps his faith unshaken. His faith is not affected even by any tragic happening. He steers clear of the whirlpool or storm that comes in life. There are many instances of such strong faith of yogis and believers in the religious and political history of the world.

Purna yogi is like a kitten, whom the mother-cat holds and picks up in her mouth and carries to the destination, unlike the young of a monkey who is to hold fast to the body of its mother. If its grip is loosened and it falls down, it is not to blame the carrier, its mother.

This yoga sadhana is higher than self-surrender. It is total surrender, surrender of all, relinquishing everything in totality, nothing remains to him.

This is a very difficult sadhana to practise. Unless one has full control over the body and mind, has developed true renunciation and has no attachment to worldly objects, how can one surrender? So this yoga is said to start at the completion of other sadhanas. It is worth trying.

11

SAHAJA YOGA (EASY SADHANA)

Many types of yoga sadhanas are mentioned in this book. Most of them require time to sit, meditate and practise, daily and regularly at a particular hour. People in the modern mechanical age have become too busy to spare time. Some have to undertake long and tiresome journey to go to and come back from office. Most of their time is spent in going, attending and coming from office. When they come back home, they are tired, exhausted and cannot concentrate. It is possible that they may also have to attend to their family, children. Sometimes it happens that a person is engaged in touring, canvassing, and selling some product and finds no rest, time and place to sit for japa or to follow other such method. When both husband and wife are employed, their household is at the mercy of a servant and their children suffer and miss adequate attention and affection from the parents. When both are tired from office work and from going and coming by bus, who is to comfort whom? Where is the time to be devoted exclusively for prayers?

If you fall under any of the above categories, I suggest you a special type of yoga system, so that you may not forget the Reality in the daily turmoil of earning your hard and honest livelihood. As a lover keeps the memory of his/her beloved in his/her heart day and night, so you may remember the Reality as often as you can, while engaged in worldly activities.

You should pause after every two or three hours, as convenient to you, for one or two minutes. Close your eyes, while sitting in a chair or wherever you are and drive all thoughts away, do *'keval kumbhaka'* (holding the breath inside and contracting the anus upward) and free the mind from work in hand:

(a) Think of God and His Divine qualities, love, mercy, truth, joy, perfection, purity etc. You may remind yourself of your real nature, feeling that you are a silent spectator of all that is happening around.

Or

(b) Imagine calmness and silence. Repeat: peace, peace, peace (Aum shanti, Aum shanti, Aum shanti). Do not look at another thought, ignore it. It is an intruder in your privacy. It is the crowd you pass by while driving in a car. If you look at the crowd you are likely to meet an accident.

Or

(c) Instead of thinking of God or Peace, or of a beautiful flower simply stand still, in void, in silence, in a state of non-reactional attention in the state of full awareness.

Any of the above three methods are not to last for more than two minutes, after an interval of two or three or four hours as convenient and possible. These are not to be tried while driving a vehicle, but can be practised while sitting in a bus or train or car. After a pause of one or two minutes, you may open your eyes, start normal breathing and resume your work in hand. You will feel a tremendous energy flowing into your body, nerves and mind. You will feel fresh, relaxed and full of calmness. You may follow this whenever you get up from the bed during night and before going to sleep, or first thing in the morning. Even if you follow other technique or *sadhanas,* you will derive great benefit from any of the above methods. It is important that during the pause, you should fully relax your body, nerves and mind.

This sadhana can be practised when your circumstances do not allow you to devote exclusively to any one of the yogic *kriyas.* You can also practise it as a subsidiary aid in addition to any regular system that you are already following. This is very easy, useful and highly beneficial technique for everyone and for all occasions.

12

HATHA YOGA

The term 'Hatha' means 'forcefulness'. It is maintained that Lord Siva, the first Lord, is the original teacher and propounder of the system of Hatha yoga. In Nath cult the practice of Hatha yoga has been carried from antiquity, and the great practitioners of this yoga have been Matsyendra Nath, Gorakh Nath, Charpati, Jalandhara, Kunedi, Chaturangi, Vicharanath, and so on. Before Matsyendra Nath, it is believed that rishi Markandeya was proficient in Hatha yoga. *Yogatattopanishad* mentions eight types of Hatha yoga. As one progresses on the path of Hatha yoga, it ultimately leads one to the Raja yoga of Patanjali.

The underlying principle of this system of yoga is that the source of thought, on the one hand and of breath and of vital force, on the other hand, is one and the same principle. Effective control of the one will naturally bring the other under control.

Yoga aims at effecting the quietening of the mind *(manolaya)*, by the quietening of the breath *(pranalaya)*, and preserving the vital energy. These are brought about by the practice of breath control, pranayama, Mudras, Bandhas and Asanas (various types of Yogic exercises and practices).

An ordinary, busy, worldly person having little time is not advised to take up this path, which is fraught with difficulties and should be followed under direct guidance and strict supervision of a living Master in suitable, congenial and natural surroundings, free from noise, dust and city pollution.

Deep, placid breathing and some easy Yogic Asanas (exercises) can be profitably practised by persons of all ages. These are convenient to do in all climates without any paraphernalia or extra expense. For a modern person, yogic asanas are most suitable, convenient and can provide much benefit in a short time.

The governing principle for the asana is to create poise, while in the process of motion. It was found that while motion generates power, a short duration of motionlessness gives manifold energy. This natural principle was discovered by yogis while watching birds, animals, plants, after whose names the asanas are named generally. This discovery by Hindu sages is the result of thousands of years of experience and experiments in the ancient times. Modern science confirms their efficacy and efficiency.

The second principle is to keep the back-bone (spine) elastic. A person remains young as long as he keeps it flexible. Any stiffness in spine will cause old age. While sitting for meditation,a yogi keeps his back-bone and neck erect. This is important. The body touches the grounds at one point and energy is not wasted while sitting erect.

As mentioned elsewhere in the book, persons suffering from certain diseases are forbidden to perform certain yogic exercises.

For the purification of the body, Hatha Yoga has prescribed certain methods:

Neti, Dhauti, Vasti, Nauli, Kunjal, Tratak.

There are four main *KRIYAS*:
Kapalabhati, Dhankani, Baghi, Shanku.

Four BANDHAS are:
Maha Bandha, Mula Bandha, Uddiyana Bandha.
Jalandhara Bandha,

MUDRAS
Maha Mudra, Khechari Mudra, Viparitakarani Mudra,
Shaktichalana Mudra, Tadagi Mudra, Vajroli Mudra,
Yoni Mudra.

SOME IMPORTANT ASANAS

Forward Bending:
Pashchimottana asana, Hala asana, Padahasta asana, Matsya asana, Sarp asana, Dhanush asana, Chakra asana, Vajra asana, Sapt vajra asana.

Side Bending:
Trikona asana, Tadasana.

Spinal Twisting:
Ardhamatsyendrasana (lateral movement of spine)

Abdominal:

Salabha asana, Mayura asana, Lola asana (mixture of Mayura and Padma).

Others:

Shirsa asana, Sarvanga asana, Urdhva Padmasana, Shavasana (relaxation).

Asanas for meditation:
Padma asana, Siddha asana, Svastika asana, Sukha asana.

PRANAYAMA (breathing exercises):

Nine main kinds of pranayama are:
Suryabheda, Ujjayi, Sitkari, Seetali, Bhastrika, Bhramari, Moorcha, Plavini and Kevala Kumbhaka .

In this chapter, I have briefly mentioned the names of important kriyas, bandhas, mudras and asanas. Interested readers may find details in many books on Yogic asanas available in the market written by Indian and foreign authors.

SOME VERY IMPORTANT ASANAS

Bhujanga Asana

Dhanur Asana

Shalabha Asana

Shavasana

Pashchimottana Asana

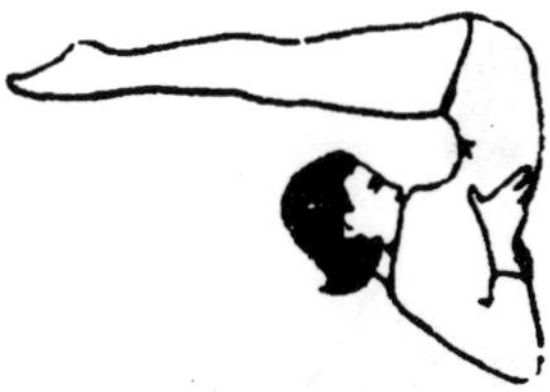

Hala Asana

Sarvangasana

Mayura Asana

Ardha Matsyendra Asana

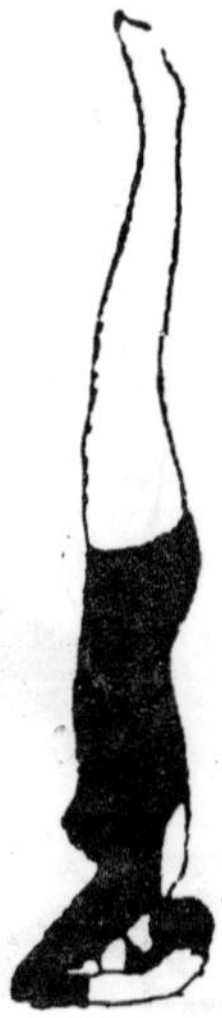

Shirsha Asana

13

PATANJALI'S ASHTANGA YOGA

Patanjali's *ashtanga yoga* includes raja yoga also. Raja yoga is a mastery of the mind, and through this yoga the mind blossoms into one-pointedness, which leads it on to the *super-consciousness.* The term *'raja'* denotes 'kingliness'; it is very precise because through this yoga a man becomes the king of mind and body.

Patanjali was a great sage, who is said to have lived in the 2nd century B.C. He codified the technique (*sadhana*) of self-realization in a most scientific and logical way. His methodical codes are universal, as they are applicable to all mankind without any consideration of caste, creed or country. It is said that his works have been translated into Arabic by Al-Biruni, and now they have been translated into other major languages of the world. Whatever systems there are in the world, as far as the spiritual discipline is concerned, they all have to borrow their basic ideas and methods from the yoga system of Patanjali. He codified and condensed the past spiritual experiences, which are rich in content and noble in reach, into his famous *Yoga Sutra*. The *Sutras* are concise and to the point. Each and every word of the *sutras* has a meaning. *Yoga Sutra* contains techniques which have been expounded in the *Katha, Svetasvatara* and *Taittiriya* Upanishads.

The preliminary limbs, that is, yama, niyama, asana, and pranayama, are aimed at ethical training and the purification of body, fine nerves (*nadis*) and mind. These are helpful in all types of sadhanas. They correspond to the well- known Ten Commandments of Moses and the eightfold path of the Buddha and the four stages of Muslim mystics, viz. *shariat,*, *tariquat, marfat* and *haqiqat*.

YAMA

(i) *Ahimsa* (non-injury) means not to cause injury to others by thought or word or deed.

(ii) *Satya* (truthfulness) means to speak truthfully in a way which does not offend others.
(iii) *Brahmacharya* (continence) denotes the preservation of the vital energy.
(iv) *Asteya* (non-stealing) means to abstain from illegal earnings, not to deprive others of their money, or of their rights.
(v) *Aparigraha* (non-possession or non-receiving) fundamentally means to be free from greed.

NIYAMA

(i) *Shaucha* means to be clean both externally and internally. External cleanliness applies to the body, whereas internal cleanliness refers to the absence of lust, greed or jealousy.
(ii) *Santosha* signifies contentment, in that one must be content both in times of comfort and strife.
(iii) *Tapas* means penance in terms of which one is able to suffer for the good, without any complaint.
(iv) *Svadhyaya* (study of the scriptures) means to have the knowledge, through texts, of the transcendent reality, whereby one is constantly remembering the divine name.
(v) *Ishvara Pranidhana* (surrender to God) means to act for Him or as His agent through body, mind and speech (thought, word and action).

Those who practice and are established in the above-mentioned ten virtues naturally reap the rich rewards in the shape of fearlessness, effectiveness of speech, attainment of wealth, healthy body and mind, and happiness. They are free from five *Kleshas* (afflictions), viz.

(i) *avidya* (ignorance), (ii) *asmita* (egotism), (iii) and (iv) *raga* and *dvesha* (liking and disliking), and (v) *abhinivesha* (will to live).

ASANAS

There are 84 asanas (body-postures) or yogic exercises. They are useful as therapeutic measures. They can avert and cure diseases: Readers are referred to the chapter on Hatha Yoga in this book.

For sitting firmly for 2-3 hours continuously, any asana—*Siddha, Padma, Svastika,* or *Sukha*—can be practised. This is required for meditation.

Sirshasana should not be practised by a person :

(a) whose blood pressure is not normal,
(b) who has weak eye capillaries,
(c) has aching and running ears,
(d) suffers from chronic nasal catarrah, and
(e) acute constipation—when stool becomes dry.

PRANAYAMA (Regulation and control of breath)

It is called *Habs-i-Dam* by Muslim saints. Breathing is the main source of absorbing energy from atmosphere. Pranayama is valuable exercise for bowels, kidneys and lungs (organs of elimination of extraneous matter from body). It gives liberal supply of oxygen to the circulating blood current throughout. The consumption of oxygen is less than normal at the time of practising pranayama and thereafter the body system works more efficiently throughout the rest of the day. It also gives massage to the heart.

The Sun is the centre of the Prana Shakti. Prana is working outside as well as inside our body and thus keeping it alive. Gross Prana moves through the physical body and psychic Prana moves in the subtle tubes or Yogic *Nadis, Ida, Pingala* and *Shushumna*. Breath is external manifestation of gross Prana.

There is connection between gross and subtle prana. It is said that our life span consists of specific number of breaths. The more a living being takes breaths in a minute the shorter is his life. The shorter the length of outgoing breath the longer the life of the person. In fact a breath is the count of the movement of life time, which is running out.

Name of Animal	*Breath Per Minute*	*Normal Life-span*
Dog	50	14 Years
Horse	35	30 "
Elephant	20	100 "
Tortoise	5	400 "
Snake	2, 3	500, 1000 "
Man	14, 16	100, 120 "

It is the experience of all of us that breathing is influenced by human behaviour and modes (e. g. anger, passion, emotion, joy, jealousy, fear, etc.) and also by food, drinks and environment. If you breathe slowly your mind automatically becomes calm. There are less waves. The practice that prevents formation of waves in the ocean of mind is 'Yoga'.

One more secret of breath—internal space has portions like navel, heart, throat and nostril and outward space is up to 16 inches from the tip of the nose. If you draw air up to the navel, you should throw it out up to 16 inches and if you draw up to heart, you should exhale up to 12 inches and if you inhale up to throat, you should throw up to 8 inches and if you draw up to the other end of the nostril, you should exhale breath up to 4 inches in length. When thoughts are renounced, the movement of breath becomes extremely slow and unperceivable.

Shiva Sambita has prescribed certain restrictions for the breath practisers such as they should avoid foods which are acidic, astringent, pungent, salty, mustard-like, bitter and fried in oil. They should not steal, bathe before sunrise, and should not harm others, be not cruel to animals or have no sexual attachments. They can enjoy clarified butter, milk, sweet food, betel without lime, camphor, a good meditation chamber with small entrance, etc.

Hatha Yoga Pradipika and Shandilya Upanishad give similar warning for gradual control of breath or practice of pranayama.

Air is oil to the lamp of life. It is the food we take through the nose. It directly feeds the mind. Mind is formed from the finest essence of the food we eat. Lest we misuse the energy produced from food, emphasis is laid on sattvika food. Energy misused is energy wasted and is against the law of nature.

I mention below a few simple and useful exercises:

(a) Pranayama is performed every morning or evening in a clean place, in fresh and pure air, in a room or preferably in a garden or on the bank of a river. Do not face the direct drift of air. Bowels should be emptied before the practice. You have to sit in Padma, Siddha, or Sukha Asana, comfortably on a *Kusha* mat, deer skin over which clean white cloth is spread.

(b) There are three movements of breath :

(i) *Puraka* (Inhalation) slowly filling the breath in lungs;
(ii) *Kumbhaka* (Pause) holding the breath. It is for a very short moment in normal case; and
(iii) *Rechaka* (Exhalation) slowly exhaling the breath from lungs.

The ratio of the above in the practice of Pranayama is to be maintained as 1: 4: 2.

Nadishodhana (cleaning of nerves): Inhale slowly from one nostril and then close the nostril and hold the breath as long as you can, comfortably. Then exhale from the other nostril slowly and hold the breath as long as you can, easily. In the second round breath is inhaled from the nostril, which remains open at the first exhalation. This practice is repeated 3- 4 times in the beginning. The ratio of time taken in inhaling, holding and exhaling should be 1 : 4 : 2 as mentioned before.

Complete Breath: It is well known that as a general rule only 1/6th capacity of lungs is used. There are four types of breathing: (a) high, (b) middle, (c) abdominal, and (d) complete yogic breath.

When breathing is done by upper part of the lungs by slowly lifting of the collar bone and shoulders and air gets in through the nose, it strengthens well the higher lymph nodes in the lungs and rest of the chest is not affected. By expanding the ribs on both sides when we inhale, we use the middle portion of the chest. It takes away pressure from the heart and gives blood to liver, gall bladder, spleen, stomach and kidneys. Abdominal breathing is done by diaphragm. Abdominal wall is raised and lowered while inhaling and exhaling, respectively. This movement regulates intestinal activity.

Complete yogic breath is taken first by expanding our abdomen, then ribs and finally raising the collarbone of the chest. This is one complete inhalation. Similarly, we draw in our abdomen first, then contract ribs and finally lower the collarbone to exhale. This complete breath removes impurities from blood and stimulates the metabolism and invigorates the whole organism.

Exercise: Stand erect. Close your eyes. Start inhaling slowly. Retain the breath after inhaling and harden your body muscles from your feet to your neck gradually, and close your fists. Retain your breath as long as you can comfortably. Your chest should expand and your belly should be pulled in. Now exhale slowly and relax the muscles of your body simultaneously, starting from your neck and going down to your feet. As you empty your lungs, you go on loosening and relaxing your muscles at the same time.

Breathing in general should be rendered quiet, unstrained, gentle, placid, and effortless in quality and slow and smooth in flow.

The foregoing four stages in Patanjali's *Yoga Sutras* are for purification of body and mind.

The three limbs mentioned below are internal and are called *Samyama*. They are related to "mind" and are consecutive stages in the process of concentration of mind.

PRATYAHARA (withdrawal of senses from objects of desires): Uncontrolled senses are like wild elephants.

DHARANA (voluntary attentiveness or concentration): It has been discussed in a separate chapter in this book.

DHYANA (meditation): Prolonged concentration *(dharana)* is termed as *dhyana* (meditation). It is like a flame. Meditation is a state of no mind. Meditation needs alert and fearless mind. Meditation is understanding of totality of life in which there is no fragmentation, no centre, and no circumference. To understand the structure of thinking is meditation.

Atma Pooja Upanishad says:

> Meditation is constant contemplation of That.
> Meditation is removal of attachment. *Sandhya*

Vimla Thakar says on meditation:

> It is a state of total being where there is no movement at all, no movement of mind, the conscious, or the unconscious. It is a state of motionlessness......... Not even the movement of awareness or intelligence, not even the awareness that you are one with universe or one with totality.

The above definition conforms with the Japanese word for meditation, "ZAZEN" which means "sitting and doing nothing, being motionless". Meditation is a living art , is existential. It is discarding the known, to be near the Unknown and that is meditation.

> "Meditation is relaxation of profound sleep in waking hours. It is effortless awareness of sleep and the waking hours together."
>
> *Sri Aurobindo*

> It (meditation) is not a smash and a grab raid on the storehouse of the Infinite, it is something that emerges from the cessation of thought.
>
> *Encyclopaedia of World Religions*

SAMADHI literally means 'completely in agreement'. It is also called Samapatti. It is a super-consciousness, cosmic consciousness or super cosmic consciousness. It is thing to be and this experience differs from person to person according to his stage of evolution. It is a state when the meditator, meditation and the meditated become one. It is a state of Bliss and Isness. It is a state of oneness with Immense Being.

Patanjali has mentioned *Samprajnata* and *Asamprajnata Samadhis*.

In Samprajnata Samadhi, mind is retained in its purity and refinement.

> Samprajnata Samadhi is the Samadhi that is accompanied by reasoning, reflection, bliss and a sense of pure being.
>
> *Yoga Sutra* I.17

> In Asamprajnata Samadhi, there is cessation of all mental activity and the mind only retains unmanifested impressions.
>
> *Yoga Sutra* I.18

In Asamprajnata, thoughts disappear in the first stage. Perfect thinking remains. Thinking also vanishes in the second stage and the state of complete vacuum, super-consciousness remains.

The above two states relate to conscious state. Patanjali also mentions unconscious Sabija Samadhi in which Unconscious is there but mind is dropped consciously. The second and higher state is Nirbija Samadhi where seed is also lost from the unconscious and there is no possibility of its coming back—there is no seed which can sprout and flower.

Swami Vivekananda in his *Raja Yoga*, has divided Samprajnata Samadhi into four varieties. He says, "It gives powers of controlling Nature."

(i) *Savitarka* : With question (i.e., sound, meaning and resulting knowledge being mixed up): Concentration on external gross elements, the state of assuming identification with gross material objects like a crystal which takes up the colour of the surrounding objects.

(ii) *Nirvitarka* : Without question (i.e., devoid of qualities, expressing only the meaning): Taking the objects out of time and space and thinking of them as they are. Knowledge of name and meaning also fade away and only the Form without name and meaning remains (in case of gross objects).

(iii) *Savichara* : With discrimination: Taking Tanmatras as object and think of them in time and space. Identicalness with abstract objects.

(iv) *Nirvichara* : Without discrimination: Eliminates time and space and thinks of the fine elements. Only the abstract without its name and meaning subsists.

Sananda Samadhi is where consciousness of Ananda continues. Sasmita Samadhi is where only the sense of abstract consciousness prevails.

Nirvikalpa Samadhi is the extreme limit of concentration, when yogi meditates upon vacant mood, leaving all external support. In this state a yogi cannot normally remain alive for more than 12 days.

The state of Samadhi cannot be described in words, as it is beyond words and thoughts. However, the most possible description of the Samadhi in words is contained in Chapter 11 of the Bhagavad Gita. Lord Sri Krishna blessed His devotee, Arjuna, with inner vision, and Arjuna witnessed the awe-inspiring Supreme power, working in the Infinite Universe. The experience of Samadhi is similar to this. Acharya Amritavaghbava had the experience of Samadhi for 9 hours at Shail Putri, Baramula (Kashmir). He told me that his experience was many times more illuminating and blissful than what has been described in Chapter XI of Bhagavad Gita.

It is a state to experience, feel and enjoy. Suffice it to say, it is a state of the highest bliss; it is a perpetual orgasm. It is human experience of oneness with God. It is something beyond time and space. Paul Brunton has tried to describe it at the end of his book *Search in Secret India*. He got into that state by the grace of Ramana Maharshi. Wordsworth has tried to describe it in his poem *Tintern Abbey* as follows:

................................That blessed mood
In which the burden of the mystery
In which the heavy and weary weight
Of all this unintelligible world
Is lightened : that serene and blessed mood
In which the affections gently lead us on,
Until the breath of this corporeal frame
And even the motion of our human blood

Almost suspended, we are laid asleep
In body, and becomes a living soul:
While with an eye made quiet by the power
Of harmony, and the deep power of joy,
We see into the life of things.

Samadhi is the ultimate aim of all methods, religions and yogas. It is meant for all. One day everyone has to reach that state, the state of union with Cosmic Consciousness to complete the circle of life.

All you have been, and seen, and done and thought,
Not you, but I, have seen and been and wrought.........
Pilgrim, pilgrimage and Road,
Was but Myself toward Myself, and your
Arrival but Myself at my own door........
Come, you lost Atoms, to your centre draw.............
Rays that have wandered into Darkness wide,
Return and back into your Sun subside.

(Ananda K. Coomaraswamy, *Hinduism* and *Buddhism*).

Instructions in yoga Aphorisms of Patanjali have been formalised by Dr. John H. Clark of Manchester University in a flow of a Diagram (Dr. Clark's article in *New Society* dated 23-7-1970). This diagram also appears in Encyclopaedia of World Religions, page 220.

14

JNANA YOGA

"He, who has fully controlled his senses, is exclusively devoted to spiritual practice and is full of faith, attains knowledge, having gained knowledge, he immediately attains supreme peace (in the form of God Realization)."

Bhagavad Gita, IV.39

It is a Yoga of Will. It is the cessation of thinking of particular and annihilation of feeling of separateness. It is a yoga of union or identification with the Absolute Existence. Yogi's puny 'self' is gone. He has merged himself with the Cosmic Whole. His realization is *Tat Tvamasi* (Thou Art That). He is living and feeling and not merely thinking or verbally repeating that Great Truth of "Thou Art That". Or the exhortations of Lord Christ. "Be Ye Perfect even as your Father in Heaven is", or "I and my Father are one".

Sri Shankaracharya, who lived about A.D. 820, expounded the philosophy of Advaita Vedanta, the cream of Vedas and Upanishads, with great clarity and competence. The teachings, summed up in few words, are as under:

There is only one Absolute Reality. What we see is Illusion (*Maya*) in the sense that it is changeable, transitory and temporary (*anitya*) and is only a part of the whole. We have not to indulge in it without understanding its nature. We have to reach the Real, the Centre, the Whole, by peeling off the covering (avarana). One Absolute manifests itself into many, as variety expresses Him excellently. So we are not to lose the sight of the Real. What we see outside and around is only a small portion of the vast, limitless, unfathomable Ocean that lies undiscovered underneath. Science has discovered that all things are composed of one substance (electrons), which is in conformity with the philosophy of Vedanta, that all is Brahman.

Matter and energy are two phases of one Reality. Matter is born of energy. Energy comes from Immense Being. Due to that interplay of matter and energy, physical universe and organic life come into being.

Man is the crown of creation. He is one with the Absolute (Brahman). But due to ignorance he confines and limits his understanding and powers. Man, who is the supreme creation and is made in His own Image, has recognised Him as Creator, Sustainer and Dissolver of this magnificent,vast, unimaginable and wonderful universe.

"Man", said Agrippa, "hath in himself all that is contained in the greater world, so that there remains nothing which is not found even really and truly in man himself", and man "also both receive and contain even God Himself. Therefore man is the most express image of God, seeing man containth in himself all things which are in God" (Encyclopaedia of World Religions).

"What is in Macrocosm is also in Microcosm".

The Jnani annihilates his 'ego', identification with body, worldly things and relations.

He actually feels that he is not the sleeping, waking or the slumbering 'self'. He realises he is Divinity himself. He is beyond mind, beyond sleep. He is the part and parcel of the Cosmos. For the attainment of the goal through this Yoga, *Viveka* (Discrimination) and *Vairagya* (Renunciation) are to be developed for the purpose of the removal of Avidya (Ignorance). *Viveka* is discrimination between the real and unreal, the temporary, changeable, transitory and the permanent (eternal).

Vairagya is renunciation from the mind of the world and the absence of emotion or agitation due to outside things, and the turning to Reality.

Shat Sampatti is six types of moral training in Jnana Yoga:

1. *Shama:* Calmness of mind.
2. *Dama:* Control of passion and senses.
3. *Titiksha:* Forbearance—cheerful endurance of tring conditions or results of Karma.
4. *Uparati:* Indifference to worldly things and relations (gladly accepting what life offers).
5. *Samadhana:* Awareness and alertness of mind.
6. *Shraddha:* Faith and devotion—success in the practice of the above will result in calmness, content-

ment, steadiness and *Mumukshutva* eagerness for liberation).

Unless the above steps are brought into actual practice in life by a jnani, he cannot say "I am that." The knowledge of "I am that" does not liberate a person. It is by dispassion and renunciation and keeping the mind in unmodified state that takes a person to the goal of liberation. It is practical and has to be brought in actual experience in daily living.

Key words for Jnana Yoga are :

Hear	— Think	— Meditate
Enquire	— Introspect	— Reason out
Assert	— Know	— Feel
Seek	— Understand	— Realise

I have given in nutshell the sum and substance of Jnana Yoga. It can be expanded and elaborated to cover a voluminous book. For more details readers may read other books by famous writers on the subject.

Himself is the pot, and Himself is the pot-maker and Himself even the clay of the Pot.

Maulvi Rumi

"All is God, all is God's
Without God is nothing"

Adi Granth Sahib

When a yogi realizes that the same consciousness is present in all bodies, without a difference, he rises above the cycle of birth and death.

Verse 77, *Vijnana Bhairava Tantra*

When a yogi perceives the universe as a magic play or as an illusion of moving trees from a moving carriage, or as a painting and contemplates over the facts, he attains peace.

Verse 102, *Vijnana Bhirava Tantra*

'Be still and know that I am God'
I hear the Master say
My heart finds rest, my fears are calmed,
He takes my cares away.

Mrs. Alfred Van De Velde

I conclude with Albert Einstein's following words:

"A human being is a part of whole called by us 'universe', a part limited in time and space. He experiences himself, his thoughts and feelings as something separate from the rest, a kind of optical illusion of his consciousness. This illusion is our prison. Our task must be to free ourselves from the prison by widening our circle of compassion to embrace all living creatures and the whole of the nature in its beauty."

15

VICHAR YOGA (SELF-ENQUIRY)

Here is a Yoga propounded by Brahmalin Bhagavan Ramana Maharshi. It is a very easy and sublime sadhana. It starts from an enquiry into the self and then peeling off one cover after the other, reaches the core, the centre of the self, the Ultimate Reality. This enquiry, appearing simple in the beginning, is full of substance and potentiality for the sadhaka (or seeker).

Sit comfortably in any Asana. Relax physically and mentally and avoid thinking—let the mind be still and silent.

Fix your gaze gently between the two eyebrows. Inhale and exhale as slowly as possible. Enquire into the Self, who am I? Am I this physical body? Consider its various parts! You will at once feel that you are not the body. The body undergoes changes of boyhood, youth and old age, yet the sense of 'I' remains constant throughout the period. The body decays and dies.

What then am I? Can I be the invisible mind, which uses this physical existence called the body? Examine the mind and its various modes, anger, fear, trust, doubt, kindness, reverence, pride etc. Am I the mind? No, the mind is also a physical organ. How can then I be mind? I use mind. I am the master. Am I then reason or faculty of discrimination? Surely not. Because when I am in deep sleep, nothing of these things exist while the 'I' notion remains and when I get up in the morning, I say "I had a sound sleep." Repeat the above questions and answers after 1 or 2 minutes ; carry on the exercise for 5 to 10 minutes to start with.

This interesting investigation of the self would lead to the rejection of the false identification of the 'I' with the body and the mind. By this dispassionate and incessant investigation, you will arrive at the conclusion, not an abstract deduction based on discursive thought, but by immediate and indubitable experience that what is real in you is Sat-Chit-Anand (Existence-Knowledge-Bliss).

One inevitable result of following the self-enquiry method will be that your attitude towards people and events will gradually change. You will begin to express qualities natural to the overself, the qualities of noble outlook, perfect justice, the treatment of your neighbour and others as your own self. Though in the beginning this method of 'self-enquiry' is a mental process, and intellectual activity, yet gradually there will be yielding up of all thoughts to the intuitive feelings which arise from within and which lead one's awareness to the Innermost:

All relations in this world are with this human body. We feel grieved due to our body relationship with wife, son and others. When a person dies or sleeps his connection with the world is severed, and he feels neither happy nor sorrowful. Thus while living in this world, if we detach ourselves from our body and mind, pleasures and pains have no meanings for us.

Because I had forsaken unity with Thee
Because I, fool, had made my body, me,
Because I did not know Thee who didst
dwell in me.

Therefore, I wandered through raging hells. Because I threw away my very self, I therefore was in chains. A vast ocean is enclosed in the Pot, and in a frame of clay (Man) heaven is hidden.

Shamas-i-Tabrez

As a handful of straw dost thou know
The body, but underneath it flows the
Ocean of life, outwardly Thou art a particle
but inwardly art Thou a hunderd suns.

Shamas-i-Tabrez

'Man' He made him in His own likeness

Bible

Know Ye that the kingdom of
Heaven is within you.

Jesus Christ

Pierce your mind with your own mind,
As penetrating as possible.
If only you sleep night and day with wise grace,
Even the stoniest of mind will break,
And become limitless space.

Tirumoolar

In the following chapter, I give short sketch of life and teachings of Ramana Maharshi, the Godman of this age, for the benefit of the readers. It will throw more light on the subject.

16

LIFE AND TEACHINGS OF BHAGAVAN SRI RAMANA MAHARSHI

The glory of India from times immemorial has been the attainment of Truth and Its application to life in all respects. The higher flights of philosophy are never the abstraction of dialectics, but the revelation of a living Truth which is the perennial source of inspiration to humanity for the expression of the noblest ideals of life.

India retains her spiritual supremacy over the world. While Mahatma Gandhi spiritualised politics and set an excellent example of Karma Yoga, there are others who worked from different planes but are not so much known to the world.

Sri Ramana Maharshi was held as one of the greatest Anubhava Jnanis of the recent times. He shook off his mortal frame on 14th April, 1950 and merged in Eternity for ever. His life will remain a Beacon Light for struggling humanity to cross the ocean of Samsara and reach the Eternal Abode. His brief life sketch and the essence of his sublime teachings is given in this Chapter for the benefit and information of the readers as well as for further research.

It was the 30th December, 1879, at 1 A. M. that the great sage came to this earth as a blessed son of Sri Sundaram Aiyar, pleader of Tiruchuzli. The day celebrated the auspicious Arudra festival, revered in India as being the day when Lord Shiva appeared before His devotees Gautama and Patanjali. He was named Venkatraman and received his early education at Tiruchuzli and Dindigul and then moved to Madura Scott's Middle School and later to the American Mission High School. The scholastic studies as such gave no sign of his future greatness. But on the playground, he reigned supreme, endowed as he was with a strong and robust constitution.

A significant event which passed unnoticed in his early age about November, 1895 was that he enquired of a relative, who happened to visit him, where he had come from? The relative replied, 'From Arunachala'. This had a thrilling and startling effect as if he had some previous understanding of the name—Arunachala, the mention of which stirred the depth of his soul with mysterious feelings.

After the lapse of about six months, one day while he was sitting alone in his uncle's house, a sudden and terrifying fear of death came over him and he felt as if he was going to die.This led him to ponder over the riddle of life and death. He began to solve this intricate problem for himself. 'What is it that dies?' He enquired within and felt that the body could not be the real 'I' existing by itself. This conclusion flashed before him as vividly as living Truth, a matter of indubitable direct experience that left him immersed in the self and not a mere intellectual process. The experience lasted for half an hour.

Thenceforward, he found little interest in his studies and drifted more and more towards the study of the self. He would prostrate before gods of Minakshi temple and pray with heart surging with emotion, eyes welling with tears for the bestowal of Divine Grace.

It was on 29th August, 1896, that his prayer was answered. It led him to foresake his home in search of the Supreme Father. He left a letter at a prominent place in the house to inform his brother that he was embarking on a virtuous enterprise, in obedience to the gracious commands of the Supreme Spirit and none need grieve or worry over this affair.

The train carried the pilgrim across rivers and rice fields to Tindivanam. Sunset found him in the temple of Araiyaninallur, where he sat for his usual meditation and had the blessed vision of a dazzling and penetrating Light within: the Higher Power spread Its benign wings to receive His earnest seeker and sincere devotee.

On the morning of 1st September, 1896, he reached Tiruvannamalai and with a bounding heart and eager eyes went straightway to the temple. He found all the gates of the temple open as if to welcome him and as it would seem strange, the whole temple was lonely. He proceeded first to the innermost shrine and prostrated at full length before it—his heart throbbing with intense happiness, sweet* tears of devotion rolling down from his eyes. A fountain of bliss gushed up into his soul and he felt himself flooded with supremely serene, tranquil and blissful vibrations.

* Tears that come out at the time of intense devotion are sweet in taste.

He came out of the temple, had the tuft of hair removed from his head; cast off his clothes, the sacred thread and the little money he possessed, and made a small strip torn from his clothes as loin cloth. His renunciation was complete. A period of spiritual ecstasy had begun, ever since he left home, and now he was engrossed in deep meditation with unbroken silence. But as some mischievous urchins made him a target for their pranks, he moved to an underground pit known as Patala Lingam. This pit was in an uncared for and insanitary condition and while he was absorbed in the self, the lower portions of his thighs were eaten away by cormon ants, leaving permanent marks on his body. He lived there submerged in the ecstasy of Divine Bliss, completely oblivious of the body consciousness.

His unparalleled austerity, his intense discipline and his pious renunciation slowly but steadily began to spread his fame like sweet fragrance of flowers, far and wide. He began to be cared for by the local sadhus. People named the young ascetic 'Saint Brahmana Swami'.

Thereafter, he had been constantly changing his abode. While the Swami was living in Pavalakunru, his mother visited him and made determined efforts to wean her son away from the sacred quest but to no avail. Appeals, upbraidings and even tears had no effect on him. On the last day she again made final effort and invoked the sympathy of other devotees present there, and eventually elicited from the swami the under-noted message, he wrote on a piece of paper:

> "The Ordainer control the fate of souls in accordance with their past deeds, their prarabdha karmas. Whatever is destined not to happen will not happen, try however hard you may. Whatever is destined to happen, will happen, do what you may to stop it. This is certain. The best course, therefore, is for one to be silent."

After the departure of his mother, he shifted his abode to Virupaksha Cave and imparted spiritual instructions to the seekers for the first time which consisted of answers to questions put to him orally. Fortunately, the manuscripts were preserved carefully by the disciples and were published under title of "A Catechism of Enquiry" and "Who am I?" Later on he composed a soul-stirring Lyric of Devotion to Arunachala.

In November 1907, Sri Kavyakantha Ganapati Muni, a well-known Sanskrit poetic genius and versatile scholar, sought the grace of Maharshi and the appeal he made to Maharshi, when by some mysterious power he was first brought to His presence, was:

> "All that has to be read, have I read. I have studied the whole of Vedanta, I have performed Japa to my heart's content, yet I do not understand what Tapas is? Hence I seek refuge at Thy feet?"
>
> "If one watches whence this notion 'I' springs, the mind is absorbed into that. That is Tapas. When a mantra is mentally articulated, if the attention is directed to the source whence the mantra sound is produced within, the mind is absorbed in that. That is Tapas".

The illuminating answer, complete and convincing, quenched the thirsty soul of the enquirer.

Thereafter, their connections grew closer and closer. Questions occasionally put by Shri Ganapati Muni and other seekers with answers given by Sri Maharshi are available as Sri Ramana Gita.

In 1908 a miraculous incident took place. While Maharshi was lying down awake, suddenly he felt his body rising higher and higher in the air and ultimately moved towards Tiruvathiyur, where it descended near the Ganapati temple. On that very day, it afterwards transpired, that Sri Ganapati Muni was staying at Ganapati temple and while engaged in meditation, he felt greatly distracted and longed to be with Sri Maharshi. At that very moment he saw the vision of the Maharshi entering the temple and placing his blessed hand over his head. Ever since Ganapati Muni proclaimed the sage as Bhagavan Sri Ramana Maharshi and he came to be known by that name. Day by day Maharshi's simple, direct and illuminating teachings attracted many disciples and admirers from all over India and abroad.

Maharshi's mother continued to pay frequent visits to her *tapasvi* son, but it was not till 1916, consequent on the death of her near relatives, that she came to live with him permanently. Maharshi then moved to a more commodious place, Skandasramam, where she passed six years of her life. On the 5th month of 1922, his mother fell seriously ill. She was attended to with matchless sense of duty and devotion by Maharshi himself. But the end seemed near. On the 19th May, 1922, Maharshi sat by her side with his right hand placed on her heaving breast and the left on her head; right from the morning till 8 in the evening when her soul was absorbed into the Infinite. Maharshi gave the Mother the transformation that was hers. The sacred remains were carried down the hill and a little shrine of Mathrubhuteswara (the Lord in the form of the mother) was built over the internment.

The Divine Will, as he once said, bade him to come from Skandasramam on the hill near the *samadhi* of his mother where he lived thereafter. Around the shrine of his mother grew the famous Ramana Ashram spontaneously. Nothing was prearranged or planned and none was asked to come and go. Devotees rendered their service voluntarily.

In 1924 robbers broke into the ashram in the hope of finding money. The Maharshi would not interfere but showed the same humility, courtesy and goodwill to the miscreants, as he would do to any other. The duty of a *Sadhu* is different in this respect from that of a *Grhastha*. He is not to give up his non-violence and so the Maharshi welcomed the blows of the robbers and counselled the inmates against resort to violence. The robbers were ultimately traced by the police and convicted.

The Maharshi had many animal companions and treated them on the same footing as human beings. He used to say "We do not know what soul may be tenanting those bodies and for fulfilment of what portion of their unfinished *karmas* they seek out our company."

Visitors from all over the world used to come to Ramana Ashram to seek the unobtrusive silence and steady outpouring of the peaceful vibrations radiating from the Maharshi, to mitigate the sorrows and sufferings of such as were worldly and to lift and elevate those whose only quest was Self-realization.

Paul Brunton, an English author of repute, got Samadhi by his Grace. Paul Brunton has mentioned this in his *Search in Secret India*. One eminent doctor, J.K. Mehta, of Jullunder whom I suggested to meet Maharshi was so much overwhelmed that he renounced the world and took to the spiritual path.

Maharshi was usually absorbed in Sahaj Samadhi. He was not mindful of his body. He had long passed the stage of body consciousness. His health began to deteriorate from 1947. In 1949, he got cancer near his left elbow. He was operated upon without any anesthesia, but was not cured. This may be the final settlement of some account. When the visitors and ashramites felt sorry and depressed on seeing him sick, he used to encourage them and would say that he would remain with them and that they need not worry. On 14-4-1950 at 8-47 p.m. his heart suddenly stopped. Hundreds of people present there at that time saw with their open eyes that a flying and shining meteor suddenly rose from the South and went behind the Arunachala peak in the North-east, exactly at the same time.

Although the Maharshi ceased to be visible in the physical body. His spiritual presence and guidance is still felt and will ever be felt by all sincere aspirants and will inspire them to higher and nobler flights in the realm of Truth and Spirit.

The Day's Programme

A programme of daily routine which was followed at the Ashram would be of interest to the readers.

Shri Maharshi used to get up punctually in *Brahma Muhurta* at 3 A.M. and with him most of the ashramities. After the morning ablutions, they gathered in the hall and while Vedic hymns were sung, they sat absorbed in meditation. The whole atmosphere was charged with spiritual vibrations, emanating from Sri Maharshi, which helped and enraptured the devotees and elevated them to the higher levels of spiritual advancement. The sunshine of Maharshi's grace was most manifest on such occasions!

The common meditation lasted for about two hours. After a short interval, they moved to the dining hall for light breakfast. By that time, visitors would begin to pour into the ashram for darshan of the sage. Noon was spent by Maharshi in imparting instructions to aspirants, answering questions from visitors, correcting proofs of forthcoming publications.

As sunset the Vedas were again chanted in the presence of Maharshi by the pupils of the Ashram with other citizens who came from the town for this purpose. At 7-30 p.m. the evening meals were served. After a period of silent meditation for about an hour in the dimly-lit hall all would retire to bed.

His Teachings

The Maharshi's spiritual attainment was supreme and complete. His presence radiated peace and his silence, the language of the soul,imparted divine wisdom. His teachings are original, direct and brief. They are practical because they are based on practical experience. His instructions, though simple, are of profound significance because they lead straight to the highest goal of spiritual endeavour. There is an ancient story of Raja Janak, who wanted to attain Brahma Vidya in the shortest time. He was illuminated by Rishi Ashtavakra by the method of 'Self -Enquiry'; which is the basis of Maharshi's teachings. He revived the forgotten Truth and taught the same in a mannersuited to the rational mind seeking to know it. No distinction is made of caste and creed and his teachings are applicable to men of all religions. There are no indispensable, orthodox ceremonies, formalities and rites to follow on the path of self-enquiry.

This then is the eternal greatness of his teachings, that they convey and express the highest spiritual Truth, realizable by direct and immediate experience, the indubitable substratum of one's own being, which is beyond thought and speech. It is the transcedental unity of Consciousness, which is also the immutable reality of the Universal Spirit. It is the supreme silence of peace which is realized as subsisting equally in all the three states of mind—the wakeful, dreaming and deep sleep. It is attained by the spontaneous, effortless abidance of the mind in the heart, and this is the significance of all spiritual endeavor, the means and end thereof.

The Maharshi had, therefore, declared that the apparent diversity of the spiritual paths did not imply any difference in the ultimate Truth, but that it is merely the superficial distinction of approach to Reality in the initial stages of practice; and that the paths of Karma, Bhakti, Yoga and Jnana are fundamentally one and the same, namely the inward plunge into the depths of one's own being, the realization of one's identity with the Self-luminous Atman.

The direct path of such realization is Atmavichar, the enquiry "Who am I?" The first and foremost of all thoughts that arise in the mind is the 'I' thought. It is only after the rise or origin of the 'I' thought that innumerable other thoughts arise. The Aham-vritti is not only the moola-vritti, but it is implicit in every other thought, for there can be no thought without a thinker. The Aham-vritti as the nucleus of the mind is called Ahankara. When the entire mind is fixed on the Aham-vritti, in order to know whence it arises, not only every other Vritti is effectively controlled, but the Aham or the ego itself is also dissolved, whereupon the One Universal Spirit reveals itself as the Atman.

The four Ashrams are merely a means to spiritual endeavour and are not condition precedent to the Atmasakshatkar (Self-Realization). The activity of a householder, who is free from attachments, is not an obstacle in the way of attaining Jnana, nor does the attainment of Jnana stand in the way of one discharging one's duties in life. Jnana and Karma are never mutually antagonistic. Indeed, it is only a Jnani that can be a good Karma Yogi and a good Karma Yogi is essentially a Jnani.

The teachings of the Maharshi, therefore, do not lay all emphasis on one path to the exclusion of the others, and on one ashram in preference to the others. Neither are they a mere theoretical synthesis of apparently divergent principles. They are the expression of the essential identity underlying the apparent diversity of the methods of approach to Reality. They are the expression of the universal eternal

Truth, he has realised spontaneously as a matter of intimate indubitable experience, which in the words of Dr. S. Radhakrishnan "does not come in a fragmentary or truncated form demanding completion by something else. It does not look beyond itself for meaning and validity. It is its own cause and explanation. It is self-established (*svatahsiddha*), self-evidencing (*svasamvedya*), self-luminous (*svaprakasa*). It does not argue or explain, but it knows and it is. It is beyond bounds of proof and so touches completeness. It comes with a constraint that brooks no denial. It is pure comprehension, entire significance, complete validity."

It is to such realization that the Maharshi's teachings give expression and to which the Gita refers:

"यं लब्ध्वा चापरं लाभं मन्यते नाधिकं ततः"

"That which when realized, he holds none other gain superior to it"

VI.22

The life of Maharshi, who had attained liberation, was not the biography of an individual but the radiance of the Universal Self, not the expression of body's acts but the manifestation of the Spirit within.

May every ardent soul in quest of Truth and Enlightenment seek and act on the sublime and supreme teachings of Maharshi and attain perennial joy and peace!

Sri Arunachala Pancharatna*

1

करुणापूर्ण सुधाब्धे, कवलितघनविश्वरूपकिरणावल्या।
अरुणाचल परमात्मन्नरुणो भव चित्तकञ्जसुविकासाय॥

Ocean of Nectar, full of Grace, engulfing the universe in Thy Splendour! O Arunachala, the Supreme Itself! Be Thou the Sun and open the lotus of my heart in Bliss!

2

त्वय्यरुणाचल सर्वं, भूत्वा स्थित्वा प्रलीनमेतच्चित्रम्।
हृद्यहमित्यात्मतया, नृत्यसि भोस्ते वदन्ति हृदयं नाम॥

O Arunachala! In Thee the picture of the universe is formed, and has its stay, and is dissolved; in this enigma lies the miracle of Truth.

* From the *"Five Hymns to Sri Arunachala"*, published by Ramana Ashram.

Thou art the Inner Self, Who dancest in the Heart as 'I'. "HEART" is Thy name. O Lord!

3

अहमिति कुत आयातीत्यन्विष्यान्तः प्रविष्टयाऽत्यमलधिया।
अवगम्य, स्वं रूपं, शाम्यत्यरुणाचल त्वयि नदीवाब्धौ ॥

He who turns inward with untroubled mind to search, where the consciousness of 'I' arises, he realizes the Self, and rests in Thee, O Arunachala, as does a river when it joins the ocean.

4

त्यक्त्वा विषयं बाह्यम्, रुद्धप्राणेन रुद्धमनसान्तरत्वाम् ।
ध्यायन्पश्यति योगी, दीधितिमरुणाचल त्वयि महीयन्ते ॥

Abandoning the outer world, with mind and breath controlled, to meditate on Thee within, the Yogi sees Thy Light, O Arunachala, and finds his delight in Thee.

5

त्वय्यर्पितमनसा त्वां पश्यन् सर्वं तवाकृतितया सततम्।
भजतेऽनन्यप्रीत्या, स जयत्यरुणाचल त्वयि सुखं मग्नः ॥

He who dedicates his mind to Thee, and seeing Thee always beholds the universe as Thy figure, he who at all times glorifies Thee and loves Thee as none other than the Self, he is the master without rival, being one with Thee, O Arunachala, and lost in Thy Bliss!

17

TRANSCENDENTAL MEDITATION (T.M.)

This fine simple method is preached by Maharshi Mahesh Yogi, disciple of Swami Brahmanand Saraswati, then Shankaracharya of Joytir Math, Himalayas. This is a most ancient technique. The method is not mentioned in any book written on the subject by the Maharshi. An aspirant is initiated in a traditional way by an authorised teacher. I had the good fortune to learn the technique from Sri Maharshi himself at Srinagar (Kashmir) and had personal discussions with him.

I here quote a parable to illustrate the method. There was a man who got control of a Jinn through the help of his Guru. The Jinn agreed to act as the man's slave on condition that the Jinn would destroy the man (his master) when the man failed to give him some work to do, as Jinn would not sit idle.

The man told him work after work and kept the Jinn occupied. The day came when the man exhausted all the list of works. According to the condition, the Jinn would not remain idle and would then destroy the man (Jinn's Master). The man was perplexed. He ran to his Guru. The Guru heard his problem patiently and told the man (his disciple) to fix a big pole in the compound of his house and ask the Jinn to climb up and come down the pole, when there was no work to do. The man came back to his house. He ordered the Jinn to ascend and descend the pole when there was no other work. So the Jinn would climb up and down when idle, and would obey orders when something real had to be done. So the man could save himself by the device.

So the Maharshi has suggested a special "thought" or 'word' to occupy the mind, when the mind is not usefully busy, or goes astray during meditation, or cannot remain silent.

A right 'thought' is selected by the teacher according to the taste and the temperament of the aspirant. The 'thought' occupies the mind for some time and then he dives deep in great relaxation, stopping activity and creating a void in the mind spontaneously cultivating a high degree of awareness. The traditional way of imparting a 'thought' (mantra) has its sanctity and importance.

The mind is just concentrated on a point, on a single thought and then directed towards its source. A real calmness and beatitude is attained, when the mind transcends the thinking process.

A thought is not perceptible as long as it is in the depth of the sub-conscious mind, like a small bubble which starts from the bottom of the pond, but as it slowly comes up on the surface, it is perceptible and becomes bigger and bigger, till it is recognised as a 'thought'. (See illustration). The T.M. practice takes the meditator into the deepest level of sub-conscious mind and expands the conscious mind and this makes the conscious mind more powerful and dominating.

The source of thought, the creative energy, thus comes within the scope of conscious mind and fills it with strength over and above the strength gained by conscious mind in fathoming the deeper level of sub-conscious.

Mind has a natural tendency to go to the field of greater happiness. When the mind reaches the state of thoughtlessneas, it feels happiness, as one feels more light when one is nearer the source of light. By the repetition of word/mantra the mind gets one-pointed and, step by step, it is led to transcendental experience.

Selection of right 'mantra' (word) is of importance as it produces certain kinds of vibrations for the individual and for other human beings. So this is left to the trained teacher to select an appropriate 'thought' (word) for the aspirant. The teacher is also responsible for checking the experience of the aspirant and the subtle states of his thinking.

Maharshi has great following in foreign countries, where facilities for scientific investigations are easily available. Such scientific investigations have revealed beneficial effect, during T.M. practice, on mind and body. *But it is certain and sure that if similar investigations are carried out in respect of other types of meditations, similar results will be noticeable.*

It is well known that by the practice of meditation breath rate decreased significantly, indicating a relaxed and restful state of nervous system, and lowered requirement of oxygen by the cells, and improved efficiency of the system as a whole.

Research carried out also shows that Meditation strengthens and immunizes the system of body, gives relief from insomnia, decreases cardiac output, indicating the reduction of work load on the heart. Skin resistance increases. (It decreases in mental tension and anxiety.)

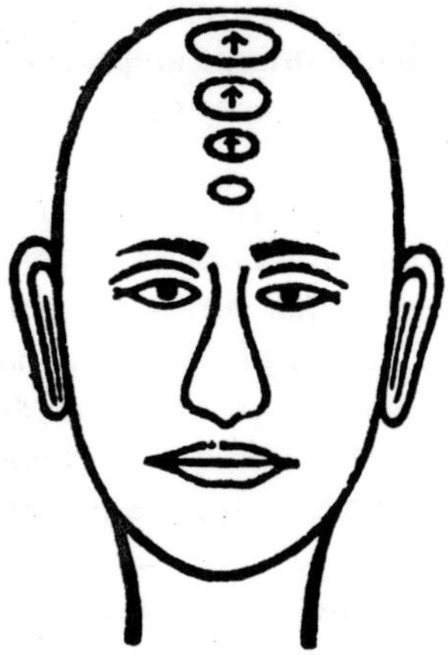

Development of thought

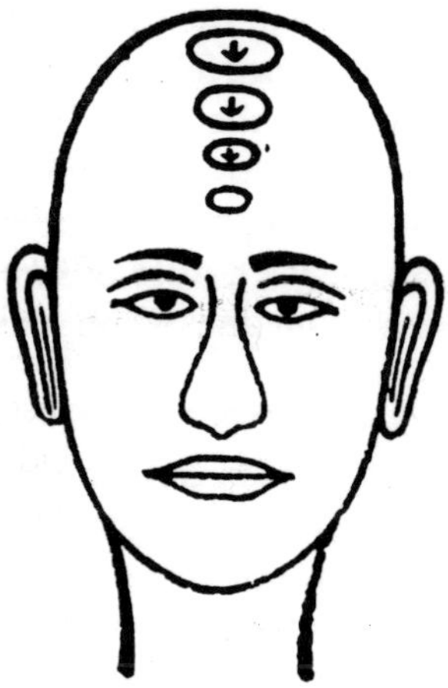

In meditation thought going deep into the subject level, until it transcends even the subtlest

Science of Creative Intelligence

When EEG is taken of a meditator, it shows an increased amplitude of alpha waves and occasional appearance of theta waves.

This proves that meditation can achieve unique amplification and unification of mental functions, which can be sustained subsequently at home and at work.

Dr. R.K. Wallace, president of Maharshi International University in Iowa (U.S.A.), who attended the *International Congress of Physiological Science* in New Delhi (India), claimed that during the practice of T. M. there is a drastic fall in consumption of oxygen as also the concentration of blood lactate. It does not happen by some manipulation in breathing pattern but as a natural physiological change. It is also claimed that the practice decreases anxiety, improves personality and creativeness and reduces weight.

The above claims are true in other types of meditations also, as already mentioned when the breath rate decreases significantly and other indications follow viz. relaxation, mental peace, tranquility, which naturally result in better mental balance, improvement in human relationship and better personality.

Certain scientific investigations were carried out recently by Dr. Mathur on Yogi Satyamurti of Govardhana, who took samadhi in an underground nine feet deep pit, in Gujranwala Colony in North Delhi on 24.3.79. He emerged alive on 1.4.79 in the presence of a large crowd. During samadhi his body temperature fell to 20.6°C and body resistance was recorded 4. 8 ohms. From the third day of his taking samadhi the ECG attached to this body showed straight line. There was no heart beat or pulse. He claims to have taken the samadhi for 280 times till then, but he did not tell me the nature of samadhi or his experience, during the period of samadhi, when I asked him.

Dr. S.K. Manchanda, Professor of Physiology, AIIMS, New Delhi, who earlier interviewed Swami Satyamurti at his place in Govardhan, told me that physical metabolism is lowered when a person goes in deep meditation. *Some Yogis can control their blood flow. They can pierce sharp needles in their cheeks, tongue or elsewhere in the body, without a drop of blood coming out. Many medical investigations have since been carried out on Yogis in trance and have been recorded.

Though the benefits claimed by the T.M. are available in all other systems, yet Maharshi considers his system* as unique and applicable

---

* Frogs and lizards hibernate during winter.

to all aspects of individual, social and political life. He has invited the governments of the world to solve age-old problems of ignorance and suffering by inculcating T.M. practice among their citizens. He thinks this will change their outlook on life. He says:

> In this meditation the mind actually experiences subtler states of thought without having to imagine, anticipate or aim at any particular process. It is an entirely innocent process which succeeds under personal guidance.
>
> The regular practice of transcendental meditation is the direct way of rising to the state of transcendental Being and stabilizing it in the very nature of the mind, so that irrespective of the mind's engagements in the conflicts inherent in the diversities of life, the structure of unity in eternal freedom is naturally maintained and life is not lost to itself. Today the fight is not between religions, or races or different ways of living, but between Spirit and Matter. Matter seems to have grown in greater glamour and has challenged the validity of the Soul. It is now for the Divine Plan to maintain the harmony between Matter and the Soul, so that real progress may be possible.
>
> Man is born to live a perfect life, encompassing the values of the transcendental Absolute—unlimited energy, intelligence, power, peace and bliss—together with the unlimited values of the world of multiplicity in relative existence.

---

* Some do not agree with Maharshi's claim about his Transcendental Meditation, saying that this cannot be a panacea for all troubles (Vide 'That Panacea Man Again'. *The Times of India,* Delhi, 3rd Oct., 1979).

18

ANAPANASATI YOGA

Like Maharshi Patanjali, Buddha has suggested the Noble Eight-fold Path:

1. Proper understanding
2. Proper aim
3. Proper use of speech
4. Proper behaviour
5. Proper mode of living (unselfish and useful)
6. Proper efforts to do good
7. Proper intellectual activity
8. Proper contemplation

All these principles are based on strict morality, selflessness, self-abnegation, and should be followed before practising the Anapanasati Yoga.

This Buddhist method is to be continuously aware of breathing for 24 hours a day. Buddha said, "even in sleep try to be aware of breathing" — continuous awareness of breathing will stop the mind, mind's movement. By concentrating on the outgoing and incoming breath, its movement is stopped.

As it may not be possible for many persons to watch the breathing whole day and night, it is better to do it for an hour in the morning. Watch your breath going in, follow it to the centre of the navel and when exhaling follow it to the Cosmic Centre outside. In between the inhaling and exhaling there is a subtle gap, an interval which is the centre. You will observe that while you are watching, you cannot think anything else. If you do, you will not be conscious of the movement of breathing.

As already mentioned elsewhere in this book, breath is prana, the vitality, the light and life in the living beings. By breathing consciously, you will create a centre of awareness and this awareness will be carried to each cell of your body. There are seventy million cells in our body—by constant and regular practice, the whole being can be surcharged with energy.

To add to this above Buddhist method of meditation, you should practice to be aware, mindful in all your actions—many actions are done unconsciously or by force of habit. But this practice is to be aware of everything you do, even while eating, drinking, bathing, enjoying sex or anything else, that is you have to be conscious of all your actions and movements. You have to live in totality in every action and in every movement of your body and mind; this will give you freedom from the subconscious, which is the storehouse of past memories and impressions *(samskaras)*.

Lord Buddha thus told his disciple, Ananda:

> "I am not asleep, only the body is asleep. I am aware and not only in sleep, Ananda, but when I will die, you will see, 'I' will be aware, only the body will die."

Muslim mystics try to remain aware and alert when going to sleep. This practice is called-Shughal-Nem-Khawabi. I quote below from Uttara Gita, supplement to the Bhagavad Gita, purporting to be subsequent discourse between Arjuna and Lord Krishna:

> See Brahman without parts, immanent at all time in the outer space.......... and in particular at the tips of the nose where the out going breath dissolves in space. Watching the breath outward following through both the nostrils, watching the point where it disappears, one should hold the mind there and meditate on Ishvara.
>
> (11-12)

> O, Radiant one, experience of Bhairava (highest Reality) may dawn in the gap between the incoming and outgoing breaths.
>
> Watch the downward and upward curves of the breath which move in a circle. Through both these turns, realise or when inbreath fuses, at that moment it touches the energy centre.
>
> When the breath is inhaled, there is a pause and when it is exhaled there is a pause-in such a universal pause, one 's small self vanishes! (*Gist of Verses* 25, 26, 27, and 64).
>
> *Vijnana Bhairava Tantra*

19

TURIYA YOGA (NIRVIKALPA YOGA) OR CHOICELESS AWARENESS

This is the ancient, quick, safe, sure and sublime sadhana taught by Upanishads. This is a jet plane method as compared to other methods, which are bullock-cart-slow moving methods to reach the Ultimate. It was first taught to me 40 years ago by Sri Amritavagbhava. He calls it Maharaja Adhiraj Yoga and mentioned it in his booklet *Shri Siddhamaharahasyam'* (published in 1969, with an introduction by Sri Gopinath Kaviraj of Varanasi). Three verses from this booklet are given below:

पद्मासनमधिष्ठाय समसर्वाङ्गविग्रहविग्रहम् ।
परस्परोपरिधृतौ करी कृत्वाङ्कगावुभौ ॥ 91 ॥

Sitting in Padmasana posture, with all limbs of the body alert, keeping both the palms, one over the other, in a lap.

निर्वातदीपवत्तिष्ठन् क्रियाज्ञनैषणाः समाः ।
अगृतहन्नत्यजन् नित्यं स्वात्मानं शुम्भुमीक्षते ॥ 92 ॥

Keeping oneself motionless like the flame of a lamp at a windless place, maintaining constantly an equally complete indifference towards taking up and doing away with all doing, knowing and willing, one sees himself as Absolute.

महाराजाधिराजोऽयं योगानामुत्तमोत्तमः
स्वशाकप्रत्यभिज्ञाने महाशाको न संशयः ॥ 93 ॥

This greatest of all types of Raja Yoga is higher even to the highest yoga systems and is highly capable to lead to the realization of one's supreme divine potency without any doubt.

This highest yoga is mentioned in 2nd and 3rd chapters of *Tantraloka* of Abhinavagupta.

Vedic seers have recognised 'Shoonya' (silence) as 'rita' which means inherent equipoise of cosmic order. Silence is derived from the Latin word 'silere' (to be quiet). It is cognate of the Sanskrit verbal root 'shil' meaning to meditate.

This 'void' theory is also expounded by Nagarjuna in his Mahaprajnaparamita shastra. His silence (shoonya) leads to no experience. For Jiddu Krishnamurti silence is creative of love, compassion and bliss. He says meditation is explosion and discovery. It is something that comes naturally when all positive and negative assertions and accomplishments have been understood and stopped. Emptiness is essential and not what is in it.

When meditator is absent, love comes into being. The mind can be silent, when it understands its own movement, as thought and feeling. It can be controlled by watching the self from a distance.

Abhinavagupta's silence (void) has several steps of elevation, briefly:

Nijananda	:	Without worry
Nir-ananda	:	Qualities of finite 'I', free from thought.
Para-anand	:	To see everything in his own self.
Brahma-ananda	:	To feel He is everywhere.
Maha-anand	:	'I' consciousness remains but no idea is there.
Chid-ananda	:	Pure consciousness
Jagadananda	:	All blissful, in union with cosmos.

Abhinavagupta does not stop at silence (annihilation of mind). He says it is only an entrance to the realm of fathomless Divinity which lies ahead.

Choiceless awareness is stressed upon by late Shri J. Krishnamurti, a great philosopher and seer of this age. From J. Krishnamurthi, other modern preachers have taken to this method, and it has become the most modern and quickest technique for God-Realization.

In this yoga the practiser becomes passive and his mind void of all thoughts, knowledge, and reasoning. He goes beyond mind in a relaxed state, without making effort. His thoughts and emotions are automatically stopped. An alert, passive and totally empty mind is capable of infinite possibilities.

Patanjali's Yoga Sutra says :

योगश्चित्तवृत्तिनिरोधः

"Yoga is cessation of the activity of the mind" (I.2) i.e. Yoga is restraining the mindstuff (chitta) from taking various forms (vrittis).

"Then the witness is established in itself -- (Sutra No. I.3) i.e. at the time (time of concentration) the seer (purusha) rests in his own (unmodified) state.

When a yogi meditates on the Void above, below and in the heart simultaneously without a thought in his mind, he will achieve oneness with the Divine.

Verse 45, *Vijnana Bhairava Tantra*

O Shakti, a yogi should visualise this universe as completely void and should completely absorb his mind in that void i.e. Siva (Absolute Reality)

Verse 58, *ibid*

A Yogi should look at the vast vacant space without tree or mountain and lose himself in that vacuity. Thus he will go beyond mind in Super-consciousness.

Verse 60, *ibid*

Sit comfortably and relax completely from top to toe. The place should be free from outside noise or any other sort of distraction, as already mentioned. You should also be at ease and have nothing to do for the time you are sitting for this purpose Nothing else should be in your mind. Now watch what is happening inside your mind, forgetting the body for the time being. If any thought comes, do not resist, do not fight, as it does not behove of a master to fight with a servant. Look at it innocently and do not associate yourself with the incoming thought. Follow it to its source, it will disappear. Learn to watch without forming a judgement or reaction as a witness in indifference. See your thoughts like a picture on a cinema screen, without attachment and without thinking or associating yourself with the story of the screen.

Totality functions only in deep passivity. It does not need effort; it needs faith. When mind is in the state of thinking, it is clouded and non-transparent. It is movement in the past or future. When thought comes either you ignore it or you can ask it 'to go', to leave you alone. Your command will be obeyed. This you might have experienced when you want to get up at a particular time in the morning. You command your mind before sleeping to awake you at a particular hour and you are awake at that exact time.

In China, Zen is practised as an offshoot of Buddhism, carried from India by the Buddhist monk, Bodhidharma. They quote example of trees which bend by the weight of snow, do not resist and the snow falls off by its own weight. The branches of the trees come to normal position thereafter. They call the method "Wu wei" i.e. no reaction to thoughts, which go by themselves, when no attention is paid to them.

Try to be non-reactional in attention. Be in perfect silence; when the mind becomes still, the body also becomes still. There is immense power in silence, in vacuum. Space* is contained in every atom. Every thought is wavering: wave becomes thought. A thought has thousands of waves. Non-wavering implies no-thought state of mind and when you are empty, thoughtless, you are at the threshold of Divinity and are about to enter into the stupendous ocean of Silence, the source of Intelligence, the realm of Super Consciousness. One has to be totally empty like a flute to welcome the flow of Divine music:

Let this Music flow into Emptiness; let Him enter and rain His blessings. You may enjoy the tender touch of Space within and the bliss of pure Isness! Void is summation of all energy.

> "Into 'thought' He comes not, even if thou thinkest million of times ...... whatever the amount has thou wit, there it availeth thee not a bit."
>
> *Guru Nanak*

---

* An Indian Scientist, Mr. Parmahamsa Tiwari, Project Engineer of Narora Atomic Power Project, has recently developed a revolutionary theory of space. His theory is confirmed by the reported development of a machine by an American scientist which extracts electric energy directly from space. Mr. Tiwari's theory is that space is not empty and is filled with an incompressible frictionless and highly mobile medium of superfluid particles, whose motion is itself the basic form of energy (*Hindustan Times* Dated 11.6.79)

As a handful of straw dost Thou know thy body, but underneath it floweth the ocean of life, outwardly thou art a particle, but inwardly thou art a thousand suns.

Shams-i-Tabrez

All else do thou turn out from thy heart so that in thy heart, nothing save God may find room.

Maulvi Rumi

Only when you are empty, you are standstill and balanced.

Khalil Gibran

Sit under the roof of the mind and Ye shall be free from the net.

To conquer the mind means to get the state of wide-awake Thoughtlessness (वृत्तिशून्य अवस्था) which will lead to self-realization.

Tukaram

Total relaxation of conditioned mind is the content of Silence—where the other energy gets activised by itself. Make room for Him to enter, when your (I - consciousness or) mind is not there, the silence reigns. Mind cannot touch the reality, the totality, as it is beyond mind and intellect. *Vimala Thakar*

The water fowl lays its beak in its breast,
and sleeps as it floats.
An old pine tree preaches wisdom,
And wild bird is crying truth
How marvellous, how miraculous,
I draw water, I gather fuel.

Encyclopaedia of World Religion

Now sink the string of
thought into the Fathomless. *Buddha*

All actions originate in rest - - This is the ultimate truth.

Leo Tzu

You know, my friend, with what a brave carcass
I made a second marriage in my house,
Divorced old barren 'Reason' from my bed,
And took the 'Daughter of the Vine' as spouse.*

*Omar Khayyam, Rubaiyat-*60

---

* Ecstatic experience.

He who realises the sphere of space hidden in the cavern of his heart grasps all that may be desired and comes into contact with the Immensity. *Taittiriya Upanishad*

Hast thou not heard His silent steps?
He comes, comes, ever comes.

Tagore

20

SURAT SHABDA YOGA OR ANAHATA

It is listening to the Divine melody. Some writers have called it Laya Yoga. It is not to be confused with Kundalini Yoga. Muslim mystics call it "Sultan-ul-Azkar" or "Shughal-i-Saut Sarmadi."

The scriptures mention that the universe was created by 'Shabda'. Muslim mystics (Sufis) say—God said "Kun" and the world was created.

आदौ भगवान् शब्दराशिः

In the beginning God was in the form of word.

Vishvasara-Tantra says :

"Para Brahman as Shabda Brahman, whose substance is all mantras, exists in the body of Jivatma. It is either unlettered (*Dhvani*) or lettered (*Varna*). The former which produces the latter is the subtle aspect of the *Jiva's* vital Shakti (power)."

Shabda is manifested in Akasha or ethereal Space. Shabda is itself Brahman.

In *Hatha Yoga Pradipika*, it is written:

"Mind is the Lord of senses, breath is the Lord of mind, and that depends on Nada."

Modern physicists consider Sound as modification of electricity and the Yogi says that electricity is the modification of sound. Sound and electricity may be two forms of one phenomenon— that phenomenon may be the primal cause. Atoms of electricity moving in a curve and in a straight line form the motion which is sound. There are many names and forms of the one Formless, for Yoga sound' is relevant, because it can be used to change the inner electricity, the mind, bio-energy.

Nadas (shabda or sound) are of many kinds. But there are two main kinds: One is Ahata—that you can produce by your efforts, by any musical instrument, or by mouth, or when one object strikes another. The other is Anahata Nada, which is produced of its own accord. It is natural and comes from within and is extremely melodious and blissful. It proceeds from the deep recesses of existence. It attracts the mind and helps the mind to attain the state of 'Laya'. This Nada exists without the medium of air unlike sound waves which travel through air.

Where there is movement, there is sound, so there is naturally a sound in the cosmos of the movement of the earth and the planets around the sun, around themselves.

In *"Shiva Sambita"*, a Yogi is instructed to close his ears with his thumbs, his eyes with index fingers, his nostrils with middle fingers and his lips with rest of the fingers of his hand and try to listen to the Mystic Sound (Anahata).

The sadhana of Anahata Nada needs particular bent of mind. I met a Yogi in Dehradun, who had developed some instrument to ascertain the state of mind and the inclination of the Sadhaka (seeker) towards the Surat Shabda Yoga.

Tyagaraja, the famous saint and musician, says, "Moksha is impossible for him who has no music in him."

Inner music is 'Onkara'/'AUM' born of the self and has Nada as its body.

In the *Nada Bindu Upanishad* the following ten kinds of sounds are mentioned:

1. Chini (like the sound of word Chini), 2. Chini Chini, 3. Bell, 4. Conch, 5. Tantri lute (an old stringed instrument), 6. Tala Cymbals, 7. Flute, 8. Bheri (drum), 9. Mridanga (double drum), 10. Thunder (of clouds).

Swami Charan Das has given some variation in the order and kinds of the above sounds but that is not important.

With the aid of a Guru, the 10th sound can be heard earlier without first passing through all the other sounds.

Hear the sound of inner Self in the following seven manners:*

1. Nightingale's sweet voice chanting a song of parting from its mate.
2. Sound of silver cymbals of Dhyanis, awakening twinkling stars.

**Voice of the Silence* by H.P. Blavatsky.

3. Plain melodies of ocean sprite imprisoned in its shell.
4. Melodious note of Vina.
5. Bamboo flute shrills in your ear.
6. Trumpet blast.
7. Dull rumbling of thunder cloud and it swallows all other sound and you hear subtle music of inner spirit.

Mystics say that the seat* of the soul is midway between the two eyebrows. It is called third eye (*Tisra Til*) *Shiv Netra* (God Shiva's 3rd Eye), *Divya Netra* (Divine Eye), *Upa Nayana* (extra eye). Muslims call it *Nuqta-i-Savaida* (the Black Spot) or *Umudimagh*.

The procedure is to shut the external nine doors (two eyes, two ears, two nostrils, mouth, anus, genital organ) and open the Tenth (Trikuti - 3rd eye, place between two eye-brows). It leads the practitioner to the Astral Plane—the unseen world. You will experience Transport and see various kinds of light such as burning charcoal, lightning, a shining star and transcendent entities and hear the sound (*nada*), as mentioned above, as you gradually advance to catch the glimpses of Divine melody ever going on within you.

Muslim mystics like Maulvi Rumi, Niaz and Khawaja Hafiz have also mentioned this Eternal Music (*Shabda*).

> The whole universe is full of this voice only if thou openest thine ears and listenest to it.
>
> *Niaz*

> Where the house of Beloved is none doth know, but only this much that from it proceedeth the music of Bell.
>
> *Khwaja Hafiz*

In this yoga the importance of Guru is emphasized. Gurus have described several spiritual lokas (Planes) (e.g. Sat Loka, Alkha Loka, Agam Loka), where the sadhaka ascends by the grace of a Guru and hears different Nadas (sounds). You have to withdraw your mind from outside and turn it inward. Then you try to stop all thoughts, and after closing your eyes and ears, you should merge your identity into the inner light and sound that you see and hear.

Agochari Mudra is closing the ears by wax and cotton and listening to the internal Anahata Sound.

---

*Bhagavan Ramana Maharshi says it is on the right side of the chest opposite to the heart

Unmani Mudra is seeing the rays of light after closing the eyes and fixing the gaze internally at Trikuti (space between two eye-brows).

Sound needs air to travel, but *shabda,* this inner sound, is a subtle transcendent entity, which reverberates in all planes above the trikuti and transports the Yogi to higher regions. Muslims call this Shabda (*Nada*) Nada-e-Asmani, Ism-i-Azam. Listening to it is called "Dhun." It is natural, universal and an easy method, and can be followed by all who are engaged in the world.

> "If a yogi listens with rapt attention to the music and to its echo vibrating even after it is stopped, he attains super-consciousness."
>
> Verse 41, *Vijnana Bhairava Tantra*

> "O, close thy eyes, ears and lips and if the secrets of God, thou dost not behold, laugh thou at me ! "
>
> *Maulvi Rumi*

> "Nectar raineth from Anahad Bani."
>
> *Guru Nanak*

> "Name is true Nectar, but what can we say?
> who mergeth in Shabda, he alone drinketh it and knoweth."
>
> *Guru Nanak*

> "Inside is the well full of nectar and by Shabda doth soul take it out to drink."
>
> *Guru Nanak*

21

KRIYA YOGA

Swami Sivananda says that Kriya Yoga is practised by Yogis who begin with some Hatha Yogic exercises and then start meditation. The initial exercises include Dhauti, Nauli, Trataka, Kapalabhati, Pranayama.

Some writers have called first part of the Patanjala Yoga Sutra as Kriya Yoga, which does not appear to be correct.

'Kriya' is derived from Sanskrit root, 'Kri' meaning to act. It achieves its goal by concentration, pranayama (breath-control) and meditation.

Dr. George Crile of Cleveland, the famous American surgeon, said that all body tissues, except the brain and nervous system, are electrically negative. The brain and nervous system become positive, because they can take up oxygen rapidly. Kirya Yoga prescribes some breathing exercises for decarbonising the blood and recharging it with oxygen.

Kriya Yoga is mentioned by Paramahamsa Yogananda in his book *Autobiography of a Yogi*. This is the real Kriya Yoga, I intend to mention. It has a special technique for arousing Kundalini and for meditation and was discovered by Mahavatar Sri Babaji, the grand Guru (Master) of Sri Yogananda. Sri Babaji's next disciple (or spiritual successor) was Lahiri Mahasaya and his disciple was Sri Yukteswar, Guru of Paramahamsa Yogananda. Their Kriya Yoga is quite different from Yogas mentioned in para 1 above.

This is a unique system of Yoga. It consists of some pranayama exercises and meditation. The technique is secret and Sri Daya Mata, the spiritual successor of Sri Paramahamsa Yogananda, can herself give initiation in Kriya Yoga or she can authorise a disciple to give such initiation on her behalf. She is the President of *Self-Realization Fellowship*. Their office is at Ranchi and Kolkata in India. Those who desire to learn the technique should write to the Society for details. On payment of fees, they supply Yogada Lessons (182 lessons)—three lessons per month—and those found deserving, are initiated into Hong-Sau* and Kriya Yoga, after taking pledge of secrecy.

One book on *Kriya Yoga* has recently come out in Hindi written by Swami Nityamuktananda, through the Divine Life Society. It contains fine exercises, and all these aim at awakening of Kundalini. Two of the exercises are given below (a few are given under Kundalini Yoga in this book). But I may mention here, that Kriya Yoga of Paramahamsa Yogananda is somewhat different from the Kriya Yoga of Swami Nityamuktananda. But both aim at awakening the Kundalini.

Exercise I: Travel from Vishuddha to Sahasrara Chakra

Sit in Siddha or Padma Asana and relax your body and mind. You have to travel in three upper Chakras in this exercise, while breathing. When you inhale you imagine to take your breath from Vishuddha Chakra to Sahasrara Chakra via Ajna Chakra. When you exhale you feel that you bring your breath from Sahasrara Chakra (top of the head) to Ajna Chakra (between eye-brows) and then to Vishuddha Chakra (front of throat). Do this exercise for a few minutes and then rest and relax.

Exercise II: Dhyana on Three Upper Chakras

Sit and relax as mentioned above. You have not to give attention to the breath in this exercise of movement of attention in three upper Chakras. Concentrate on Vishuddha Chakra situated in the region of the throat in the spinal column, as a lotus with 16 petals of sparkling blue colour. Then slowly shift your attention to Ajna Chakra (between the two eye-brows) as a Lotus with two golden sparkling petals. Lastly bring your attention to the Sahasrara Chakra and visualize it as a Lotus with innumerable petals of varied colours mixed with red. By such visualization in the start on each Chakra, you will advance further and will begin to see actual colours in the Chakras at their respective places. Do this exercise for a few minutes and then rest and relax.

*'So Ham' see Chapter on Ajapajapa.

22

KUNDALINI YOGA, CHAKRABHEDA YOGA OR SIDDHA YOGA OR LAYA YOGA

सशैलवनधात्रीणां यथाधारोऽहि नायकः
सर्वेषां योगतंत्राणां तथाधारो हि कुण्डली ॥

"As of all with hills, woods and lands, the support is Lord of serpents, so of all treatises of Yoga, the support verily is Kundalini."

Kundalini Yoga is of great scientific, para-psychic and metaphysical interest. It is called 'Laya Yoga' (Laya means absorbing) and Kundalini means 'coiled up'. It is also called 'Serpent power'. This was recognised 5000 years ago and is mentioned in ancient Hindu scriptures e.g. *Saundarya Lahari, Panchastavi, Yogakundali Upanishad, nanarnava Tantra, Lalita Sahasranama, Laghu Stuti, Vamakesvara Tantra, Yogasikha Upanishad, Gheranda Samhita, Shatchakranirupana, *Hatha Yoga Pradipika*. From the above scriptures, knowledge spread to other countries and religions. It is mentioned in the ancient scriptures and findings of Tibet, Egypt, Sumer, China, Greece, Mexico, and South America. A German mystic in Europe, Johann George Girchtel, has given an account of the Chakras in his book *Theosophia Practia'* issued in the year 1696. In Rasala-i-Haq-Numa, by Prince Mohammad Dara Shikoh, three Chakras (Lotuses) have been mentioned as *Dil-i-mudawar, Dil-i-Sanowbiri and Dil-i-Nilofari*.

In the human body, Kundalini is the basic energy, the creative force, a primal cosmic energy outside electromagnetic spectrum, lying dormant in Muladhara Chakra (Plexus). This energy is also permeating the whole universe and the universal Kundalini is called "Maha Kundalini."

* Its English translation is available as 'Serpent Power' by Sir John Woodroffe.

What is present in Macrocosm is present in Microcosm. Man is epitome of the Universe. In 1619, Robert Fludd demonstrated such interconnection between man and universe by drawing seven circles around man.

Kundalini (individual static form of creative energy) is the mother of Prana. Prana is vayu or universal force of activity.

There are two aspects of one Supreme Absolute, manifested and unmanifested, Power-holder and Power, seen and unseen, positive and negative, changeless and changeful, Shiva and Shakti, Krishna and Radha, Vishṇu and Lakshmi, Rama and Sita, Brahman and Maya, Formless (Nirguna) and Saguna (with Form). In Sankhya Philosophy, these are called Purusha and Prakriti. In China they are called Yang and Yin (Passive and Active). Thus one Supreme is beautifully represented by Ardha-Narishvara in Hindu mythology. They are also called Poise static and Poise dynamic. They are inseparable like fire and heat. There is no Power-Holder without the Power and no Power without the Power-Holder.

Kundalini represents the feminine energy (*Shakti*), which is always trying to unite with her master, Sadashiva (Cosmic Consciousness) in Brahmarandhra (*Sahasrara*) situated in brain, ventricular cavity.

Shri Vasant G. Rele has said in his *Mysterious Kundalini* that it is right vagus nerve which supplies and controls all important organs through different Plexuses of the sympathetic portion of the autonomic system (over which we normally have no control). In the Foreword of the same book, Sir John Woodroffe (Arthur Avalon) does not subscribe to his (author's) view. He says it cannot be a nerve or any other physical substance or mental faculty, but the Ground Substance of both, which, on being aroused, ascends and is merged in Higher Tattvas, ending in Shiva-Shakti Tattvas, when she is said to be merged in Parama Shiva.

Vamakesvara Tantra says that all the Chakras are in the subtle body (*Linga Sharira*). Shri Aurobindo has mentioned Kundalini in his famous 'Savitri' as cosmic Energy.

Late Pt. Gopikrishna says that Kundalini can be scientifically verified in a laboratory to prove the ancient truth and that the seventh Chakra (Sahasrara, 1000 petal lotus) is entire brain, as after the entry of Kundalini, the whole cranium is illuminated and a new pattern of consciousness is born. He has not mentioned any method for awakening this Serpent Power in his books. In my personal dialogue with him, however, he told me that any method can be employed. Some methods are given in the Bhagavad Gita. Awakening of Kundalini is an evolutionary process and should come in a natural way. He preferred easy methods, moderate living and natural awakening of Kundalinion one's spiritual maturity.

Modern anatomy, however, does not confirm the existence of Ida, Pingala, Shushumna or seven Chakras (plexuses) in human body, as claimed by Kundalini Yoga.

Chakras are not in gross body (*annamaya kosh*). They are subtle force centres in the ethereal duplicate or astral body. Acharya Amritavagbhava says, Muladhara Chakra is like an electric meter in the body. It supplies energy to the body and mind according to their requirements. Sahasrara Chakra has connection with Universal Kundalini (*Maha Kundalini*) and when a yogi reaches that Chakra, he attains immense powers and *Siddhis*.

It is also said that Kundalini is to man as a coiled spring is to a watch. Kundalini keeps the count of breathing, pulse and heart-beat and when the allotted number of breaths have finished, life stops. Kundalini also converts stored up Karmas into Karmic events. It is principally responsible for maintaining body temperature.

It is laid down in the scriptures and confirmed by many yogis, seers, clairvoyants [1] that Kundalini is present in Muladhara [2] Chakra (pelvic plexus), Yukta Triveni, in the shape of a sleeping serpent, forming three coils and a half, bathed in saffron luminous colour like a streak of lightning, like a body made of pure shining gold, and is coiled around the base of human spine. It is in a circular shape enclosed in a triangular base (coccyx). It is psychosomatic power centre. The subtle channel or nadi (stream) which starts from Muladhara (pelvic plexus) or from the right scrotum according to some texts, goes up alternating from left to right and from right to left, around the spinal cord and lotuses, and reaches the Ajna Chakra (Mukta Triveni), makes a plaited knot of three and turns towards the left nostril and is called Ida (Ganga). Similarly the subtle channel (stream) which starts from Muladhara Chakra (or from left scrotum according to some other texts) goes up straight alternating

1. For example, well-known theosophists, Mme. H.P. Blavatsky, C.W. Leadbeater, Rudolf Steiner and many others. Swami Muktananda, disciple of Sri Swami Nityananda, a great yogi, is reported to have awakened Kundalini in several of his deserving disciples, by his graceful touch (*Shaktipata*).

2. Mula means root, and adhara means support. It is exactly in the middle of the human body.

from right to left and from left to right, enters Ajna Chakra, makes a plaited knot and turns to right nostril and is called Pingala (Yamuna).

The Prapanchasara Tantra says that these Ida and Pingala are bent like bows from the shoulders.

The stream ending in right nostril (Pingala-Mihira) is Surya Nadi and is of red colour which produces heat in the body and is masculine (*Rudratmika*).

Ida (or Lalana or Sasi) is Chandra Nadi, is of yellow colour, produces coolness and contains nectar. It is feminine in character and is Shakti-Rupa.

Sushumna (Sarasvati) is the central Nadi and starts from the inside of Kanda or Muladhara (the root of all Nadis), and goes to the end of the neck (Sahasrara) through the hollow of the spinal column, clinging to it like a Chavya-creeper, crossing the five Plexuses (Nerve Centres or Chakras). She is fiery, red and is the container of 'Citrini',[1] which is the subtle channel inside Sushumna—the embodiment of 'AUM'.

Kanda means bulb. It is junction of over 72 nerves. In all, there are $3^{1/2}$ crores of nerves (nadis) in the body.

This Plexus (Muladhara) is about $1^{1/4"}$ below the penis and $1^{1/4"}$ above the anus (Perineum). It has a shape of a bird's egg and is about $2^{1/4"}$ in breadth, broad above and narrow below, covered with soft, flimsy, white substance. It has four petals (Petals indicate radiation from the particular Astral centre or Lotus).

The breath flows from each nostril (left and right, Ida and Pingala) alternately for about one hour in a normal course, during day and night. On the 1st, 2nd, 3rd, 7th, 8th and 9th, 13th, 14th and 15th of every bright fortnight, breath flows through left nostril. On 4th, 5th, 6th, 10th, 11th and 12th of the same fortnight, it flows through right nostril. On similar days in dark fortnight the flow of breath is reversed.

The flow of breath from right or left nostril, as mentioned above, is counted from the time of sunrise.

You can change the flow from right nostril to left if you lie down on right side and vice versa. When the breath flows from both the nostrils, it is moving in Sushumna (Sarasvati) Nadi. All Yogis want to prolong the flow from Sushumna Nadi at the time of meditation, as it helps in concentration and awakening of Kundalini.

---

1. C(h)itrini is subtle like spider's thread, pierces all the Lotuses in the back-bone and is pure Intelligence.

There is a science of breath (*Svarodaya Vijnana*) which is in itself a vast subject. It is beyond the scope of this book to deal with it.

According to medical science, the respiratory act is under the control of Vagus Nerve, which has two sets of fibres, afferent (i.e. incoming) and efferent (i.e. outgoing). Stimulation of the first (afferent) stops expiration and produces inspiration and the stimulating of the second (efferent) does the reverse. Afferent current is sensory and centripetal. Efferent current is motor, centrifugal. One carries impulse to the brain and the other from the brain to the outer body.

The awakening of Kundalini creates motion and motion creates sound which is called 'Nada'. Nada creates light. The Light appears as Maha Bindu. The sound of creation is AUM—which is also called Shabda Brahman. From AUM are produced 52 letters of Matrkas, letters in their subtle and causal form. Out of these 50 odd letters, fifty-first is light, and fifty-second a current of light.

When Kundalini is awakened, it travels from Muladhara chakra to higher up, passing through Svadhisthana, Manipura, Anahata, Visuddha, Ajna and ultimately uniting with Sadashiva in sahasrara (called 1000 Petal Lotus).* As she ascends to higher chakras (plexuses), she gains powers of various spheres and control over Tattvas. (See illustration).

Each Chakra has a specific shape, word (bija mantra), deity and loka. Awakening of a Chakra gives super-natural powers to the yogi pertaining to that particular Chakra. Each Chakra is divided into positive and negative half. This causes twelve signs (*rashis*) of Zodiac. Each planet owns two signs except sun and moon which are luminaries.

There is disagreement among writers about the colour ofChakras and number of petals in each Chakra. Petals represent number of powers associated with each Chakra. Each Chakra (centre) is connected with state of matter i.e., earth, water, fire, air and ether, indicating different planes e. g. physical, astral, mental etc. Chakras are symbolic. In each Chakra there is an animal figure, two deities (male and female) and particular Sanskrit letters representing phonetic sounds. Animal figures denote elements. Feminine divinities show powers governing various bodily substances.

Kundalini may be awakened by different methods. A Hatha Yogi may do it by Pranayama (Breath-control), Asanas, Mudras (yogic pos-

---

* Not exactly 1000. It means innumerable. C.W. Leadbeater says there are 960 petals according to his experience.

tures), a Raja Yogi by meditation on 'Self', a Bhakta (devotee) by shraddha (faith) and devotion or by self-surrender (samarpana),a Jnani by will power, concentration on the self leaving body consciousness, a Tantrik by sex sublimation and Siddha Mantra (repetition of formulas). It is awakened sometimes by Grace of Guru (master) who can kindle the fire in very deserving cases. Guru's Grace is also needed for progress on the paths. Some use drugs, herbs to stir it into motion. It is said that in China, some herb (Kesar, saffron) is injected in the spinal cord for this purpose. When Kundalini moves up in higher Lotuses, a Yogi gets *Siddhis* (supernatural powers. When Kundalini joins Paramashiva in Sahasrara Chakra, the Yogi gets Samadhi, enlightenment. He floats in the ocean of Eternal Bliss, indescribable in words, as the state is beyond words, thought, time and space.

Mind, Prana, Jiva ascend together to higher lotuses along with Kundalini. Intense devotion and prostration and prayers unto the Divine Mother can help the sadhaka (practitioner).

Fruits which ripen on trees are sweeter and more delicious than those plucked raw and ripened by artificial method. Similarly trees which take longer time in growing, produce better kind of wood. Therefore, any effort to force the awakening of Kundalini is harmful. Many instances of mental imbalance are reported by forceful and hurried methods. There is a great danger in premature awakening. The receptacle should be ready to receive the tremendous upsurge of the energy.

> Sri Aurobindo says that as higher and deeper consciousness dawns upon a sadhak, there is effortless blossoming of the Lotuses. The hidden centres of the celestial force open like flowers in a heavenly atmosphere. As if a fiery kiss had broken their sleep, they blossomed and laughed, surcharged with Light and Bliss.
>
> *Savitri*

There are four paths open to Kundalini to reach Sahasrara (1000 Petal Lotus), one is from front, the second is the longest from the backside of the spinal cord (used by Sri Shankaracharya). The third is from Anahata (Hridaya-Heart) and the fourth is from Ajna (place between two eye-brows).

When Kundalini Shakti ascends upward, it does not leave a void at the base (Muladhara Chakra). Static energy remains there.

The position of endocrine glands in our body may have some bearing on the position of Chakras (Plexuses):

Sex gland corresponds to Muladhara Chakra
Suprarenal corresponds to Svadhisthana Chakra
Pancreas corresponds to Manipura Chakra
Thymus corresponds to Anahata Chakra
Thyroid and Parathyroid corresponds to Visuddha Chakra
Pineal corresponds to Ajna Chakra
Pituitary corresponds to Sahasrara Chakra

Seven Chakras (mystic centres) in the human body

From bottom to top:

1. Muladhara Chakra
2. Svadhishthana Chakra
3. Manipura Chakra
4. Anahata Chakra
5. Visuddha Chakra
6. Ajna Chakra
7. Sahasrara Chakra.

A description of seven chakras is summarised in the table on the next pages.

Awakening of Kundalini brings peace, tranquility, contentment, power of self-control, faith in God, devotion, sweet voice, lustre in the eyes and body, freedom from fear and worry.

Sl. No.	Name of Chakra	Situation in Spinal Chord	No. of Petals*	Tattva & Its Quality	Colour	Symbol	Seed Utterance@ (Bija Mantra of Element)	Devata**	Shakti	Loka	Planet Sign (Rashi)
1	2	3	4	5	6	7	8	9	10	11	12
1.	Muladhara	above the anus and below organ	4	Earth sense of smell	Yellow	Square	Lam लं	Brahma on Hamsa	Dakini	Bhur (Physical	Saturn 10, 11
2.	Svadhis-thana	above genitals	6	Water sense of taste	White	Crescent	Vam वं	Vishnu on Garuda	Sakini	Bhuva (Vital)	Jupiter 9, 12
3.	Manipura	Front of navel	10	Fire (Tej) form & colour	Red	Triangle	Ram रं	Rudra on Nandi	Lakini	Sava (Mental)	Mars 1,8
4.	Anahata	Front of heart	12	Air (Vayu) sense of touch	Smoky	Hexagon	Yam यं	Isa	Kakini	Maha (Intellectual)	Venus 2,7

5.	Visuddha	Front of throat	16	Ether (Akash) sense of hearing	White	Circle	Ham	Sada Shiva	Sakini	Jana Super-(Intellectual)	Mercury 3,6
6.	Ajna	Trikuti	2	Manas hearing (mental faculties)	Golden		Aum	Sambhu	Hakini	Tapa Spiritual	Sun 5 Moon 4
7.	Sahasrara	Head	1000	Atma	Colorless light		Avyakta Pranava	Kameshwari & Kamanatha Paramshiva Para Shakti		Satya (Divine)	

* Sanskrit letters on petals are not mentioned here.

** In some works Ganesha is the God of Ist Chakra, Brahma of the 2nd and Vishnu of the 3rd.

@ Bija mantra is recited in doing Puraka (inhalation), Kumbhaka (retention) and Rechaka (exhalation) pranayama in the following ratio:

4, 16, 8 = 28 (Adhama) lower stage
8, 32, 16 = 56 (Madhyama) middle stage
16, 64, 32 = 112 (Uttama) higher stage.

A few safe exercises (techniques) for awakening the Serpent Power are mentioned below. The practice should be started under the guidance of a living master :

1. While doing pranayama, fix your gaze at the tip of your nose. It will stimulate the afferent sympathetic system and will affect Kundalini, as convergence of the eyeballs to the nearest point in the body takes place and stretches the lateral rectus muscles of the eyeballs, and stimulates the ciliary gangilia, which are in close connection with them in the orbit.

2. Sit in Siddha Asana (keeping the left heel under the anus and placing the right heel above (both the ankles should be one upon the other). The perineum (yoni) is pressed with the heel. Spine and neck are kept erect and hands are placed on the knees. Practise Mula Bandha, Jalandhara Bandha and Uddiyana Bandha (all together in one rhythm constitute Bandha Traya). Mula Bandha is practised by contracting of anus upward, while you start deep and prolonged inhalation. After inhalation is completed, breath is retained as long as comfortably possible in Jalandhara Bandha, by pressing the chin against the root of the neck. Then you start exhaling and contracting the pelvis (lower abdomen) till it is completely flattened. This is called Uddiyana Bandh. Mula Bandha and Uddiyana Bandha help in preserving the semen. Jalandhara Bandha absorbs the flow of nectar from the Sahasrara Chakra. All three Bandhas aid in awakening of Kundalini.

Khechari Mudra

In this mudra, tongue is lengthened, sometime by giving a small cut, weekly beneath the tongue (fraenum) at its joining point (one hair's breadth in seven days). The cut is treated with honey and turmeric. This is done by a Guru (Master adept in this Yoga) and not by a surgeon. The tongue is turned backward and put behind the posterior nasal opening. Gaze is fixed on the root of the nose. Thus the tongue licks the nectar, falling from Brahmarandhra, which is normally consumed by the fire in the navel. This mudra is to be done in the presence of a Guru. The yogi tries to absorb the energy within the body by blocking the opening of the lungs by rolling up the tongue. It is to gain control of Kundalini.

Maha Veda

It is combination of Bandha, Turya and Tandan Kriya. In the morning, after clearing the bowels, on an empty stomach, sit in Padma asana in Maha Bandha, with your back and neck erect. Contract the anus and draw in *apana vayu* upward. Breathe slowly and retain the breath inside by doing *Jalandhara bandha*. Press the chin against the chest. Keep your palms on the ground and raise your buttocks slowly on the hands and palms and then bring it down slowly to your seat, keeping the asana intact and firm. Some texts suggest striking of the posteriors on the ground, after raising them. This will purify the body nerves, stop decay and stir the Muladhara Chakra.

Chakras

Sit comfortably and relax physically and mentally—be at peace with mind and body—breathe slowly, deeply and rhythmically without any sort of jerk If a thought comes, ignore it. Do not get angry or try to suppress it. It will pass away when you are watchful. Now take the breath from Ajna Chakra to Muladhara Chakra staying momentarily at each midway Chakra, i.e. at Vishuddha, Anahata, Manipura and Svadhisthana through the spinal column. Retain your consciousness at the Muladhara, imagine the triangle surrounding the serpent power of Kundalini with tail upward and mouth downward. Now inhale and move your breath in imagination from Muladhara Chakra through the spinal column and the six chakras, i.e. retain the breath consciousness at the base Chakra and fixing the gaze at the Ajna Chakra, you should move your attention and breath from Ajna Chakra to Muladhara Chakra and ascending from Muladhara Chakra to Ajna Chakra while exhaling and inhaling respectively.

You have to do it with intense attention and awareness. It will make you conscious of the dormant dynamic force lying in you and awaiting and deserving your whole-hearted attention. Power of manifestation is inherent inside Kundalini but it awaits proper time according to the spiritual development of the aspirant, his urge, his past and present *Karmas* (efforts) and last but not the least the Divine Grace.

Tantra says Kali, one of the ten great Cosmic Powers, is Kundalini in the body, expressing herself as activity through *Prana shakti*. Her grace is gained by fixing one's consciousness constantly on breathing as mentioned in the chapter on Anapanasti Yoga in this book. Her Bija Mantra is 'KRIM'.

Concentrate on the Prana Shakti (vital energy) arising from Muladhara (Pelvic Plexus) like rays of sun or like lightning and merging in Sahasrara (1000 petal lotus) in the pericap directly or by passing successively through other plexuses (chakras) in between. In both cases a yogi attains Divine Consciousness.

Vijnana Bhairva Tantra, Verses 28, 29

Seated with closed eyes and inwardly concentrating one's mind on union of Siva and Sakti in the centre of the brain, gaining mental poise, one can reach the supreme Reality.

Verse 34, *ibid*

If one concentrates on the void in the sushumna (middle channel) which is slender like lotus stem, one can attain Divine Consciousness.

Verse 35, *ibid*

OM, AIM, KLIM, STRIM

॥ ओं, ऐं, क्लीं, स्त्रीं, ॥

23

TANTRA YOGA—YANTRAS AND CHARMS

There is a solitary reference to Tantra in the Rigveda. It literally means agricultural implement (loom or plough which is 'spread out').

In the *Mahanirvana Tantra*, Lord Shiva promulgated the teachings of Tantra in the form of talk between Him and His Consort, Parvati, the Great Divine Mother, on Mount Kailash, in response to Her enquiry about the most appropriate Shastra in Kaliyuga.

In the *Gayatri Tantra*, it is mentioned that Lord Ganesha preached Tantra vidya to the Devayoni on Mount Kailash after learning it from Lord Shiva.

It is claimed that Tantra is the Shastra in Kaliyuga for attainment of life's goal, as were Sruti and Vedas in Satyayuga (Golden Age) and Smriti in Tretayuga (Silver Age) and Puranas in Dvapara Yuga (Copper Age).

In Kaliyuga, Dharma (Righteousness) has decreased to a quarter from full stature in Satya Yuga. In every Yuga it decreased. But length (duration) of Kaliyuga also decreased by 1/4 of Satya yuga, 1/3 of Treta yuga and 1/2 of Dvapara yuga.

Vedas are Mulashastras (original scriptures) and all other Shastras (scriptures) are based on them. Tantra is claimed as the fifth Veda.

From the excavation in the Indus Valley it is proved that Tantra Yoga was known to the residents of this Valley more than 3000 years before the birth of Christ.

Tantra has recognised different temperaments and natures of human beings and has prescribed different modes and techniques for each category of persons. Everything in nature has been classified as sattvika (harmonious, orderly), rajasika (active and restless) and tamasika (material and sluggish). This is confirmed by modern science. On the basis of three tattvas mentioned above, *Tantra Shastra* has classified human nature as pasubhava (animal type), virabhava (hero type) and divyabhava (godly type). One can progress from lower type to higher type. The aim of Tantra is to attain Dharma, Artha, Kama and Moksha. Dharma is religion, piety, morality. It consists in right thinking, right living and right action. Kama is desire for wealth, success and woman. Artha is wealth by which life can be maintained i.e. food, drink, houses or high desires for worship etc. Moksha (Mukti) is liberation—the ultimate aim of human existence.

M.P. Pandit writes :

> "The Tantra is the breath of Divinity and the world is evolved from the breath. The Divine Mother (Call Her Father or Father-Mother as you choose) is in every molecule, in every atom, in all things that constitute the world. In fact She is causeless Cause of whatever is; She is manifested Brahaman. The world is playground (Lilakshetra) of the All Blissful Anandmayi. World is neither an illusion nor a non-reality."

The Tantra sadhaka, by his method of worship, is made at the outset to feel and then by higher process of self-culture, to realise All-Blissful-Mother, in the universe. Nothing is condemnable. Purpose of life is to live with life but with an inner awareness. There is life around and life within. Universe is the expression of the Absolute. It reveals Him, if correctly perceived, and does not veil Him.

As we breathe in and out, similarly there is eternal rhythm of Divine Breath—outward breath is from the spirit to matter and inward is back from matter to the spirit. Outgoing (extrovert motion) is called Pravritti Marga (seeking enjoyment in the world) and inward (introvert motion) is called Nivritti marga, which seeks everlasting happiness in union with the Absolute (Primal Source).

The Shakti is both desire and the light of knowledge and the person who has enjoyed the world knows by experience the futility of such enjoyment. Tantras emphasise the absolute control in outward movement, as a general rule, as is followed by the aspirants of other Yogas.

Tantra Shastra is verifiable at every step. It gives results. It is Encyclopaedic Science. It is a technique. It is open to all irrespective of caste, creed or sex. It is not confined to any religion. The world is considered as material and field for Sadhana—rightly understood it paves the way to reach Brahman (Absolute).

Tantra Yoga is based on psycho-physical discipline. Adepts in this

Yoga have by centuries of experience and practice perfected it to its fullest potential and ensure rapid success in liberation of the human soul.

Tantra Shastra firmly believes in the Law of Karma. There are two paths—one is called Vama Marga (left-hand marga or Kaula Marga) and the second is Daskhina Marga (right-hand path or Samaya Marga).

One of the basic principles of the left-hand method is to gain by its practice both liberation and enjoyment. This can be possible by identification of the individual self, while in the state of enjoyment, with the Universal Self. The power of passion when controlled can overcome man's baser nature. It has the force to keep a man free from the worldly bonds.

> Enjoyment is the grasping of the form of what is perceptible. It is the realization of the quality of what is desirable or undesirable.
>
> *Yoga Sutra-bhasya of Vyasa*

In Vama marga the gross animal tendencies which are visible in eating, drinking and coition are made the basis of practice. These functions are subject of Pancha makara or Pancha tattva. There are madya (wine), mamsa (meat), matsya (fish), mudra (parched grain) and maithuna (coition or lata sadhana).

These are used only after purification in Tantric worship in the prescribed manner. It is forbidden for Pasu (lower grade). Maithuna is allowed with householder's own wife. Tantric Maithuna is not ordinary coition. The whole process is done consciously and voluntarily and does not end in emission of vital fluid by copulation. Those who do not understand the basic principle of this sadhana, have defamed it.

According to scriptures, the union of husband and wife should take place once a month on the fifth day after the cessation of menstruation. Tantra stresses the importance of a competent sadhaka (adhikari—deserving student) for such rituals, which are performed in a group and in the presence of a Guru, under his guidance and strictly according to the rules laid down for such sadhana.

The five of the above elements act as poisons in this world for the spiritual progress of a person. So Tantra has used them to eradicate them. Poison is an antidote to poison. Diamond cuts diamond and the Law of Similars *(similia similibus curentur)* in Homoeopathic treatment is well known. Great care is taken to treat a patient with precise doze of poison, as any wrong or excess dose can kill the patient. It is laid down in the *Mahanirvana Tantra* that in Kaliyuga as the householders' minds are much attached to the worldly things and are not under control, three sweets (milk, honey and sugar) should be used in place of wine and the fifth Tattva should be accomplished with worshipper's own wife, in the ritual.

Five Tattvas are also defined as the five Pranas and five Maha Pretas and they denote: (1) drinking of the wine of Divine intoxication, (2) control of flesh (body), (3) being aware of the 'self' while moving and acting in this world like a fish or a lotus in a pond, which always remains above the surface of the water, (4) killing of egoism, (5) union with God.

Yogini Tantra says that the union of Shakti Kundalini with Shiva in Sahasrara Chakra of a devotee is the best union (Maithuna). According to the *Agama Sara,* wine is the somadhara or lunar ambrosia, dropping from Brahmarandhra (brain) which the fire in the navel licks up. So a yogi practices Khechari Mudra by closing the opening in the throat, with his tongue turned upward, to stop the nectar from falling and being burnt up. Meat (mamsa) is the tongue (Ma), Matsya (fish) are the two Nadis, Ida and Pingala. The Yogi controls these nadis by Pranayama, eats them by retention of breath (Kumbhaka). Mudra is awakening of the knowledge in Sahasrara Lotus, the seat of Atma (Cosmic Consciousness).

The vulgar practices that crept in Kula Marga were reformed by crusades started by Shri Samkara Bhagavat Pada. In view of beautiful methods of Samaya doctrine, unique and famous hymns, *Saundarya Lahari* (*The Flood of Beauty*) and *Panchastavi*, came into being, in praise of Maha Shakti (Divine Mother).

Dakshina Marga is a path which teaches the method of Japa of Mantras, Tantras and Yantras with a mathematical accuracy. Tantra Yoga is Mantra Yoga, Japa is done in a prescribed manner with precision, concentration and devotion for the accomplishment of one's desires, worldly or spiritual or both. Graded system of Sadhana is given according to the competence of the sadhaka.

Mental Japa is performed. Mantra may contain the seed (Bija) Mantra. Mantra is the sound body of the deity. The word Mantra means thought-form. By understanding of the inner significance of the mantra, we can realise the nature of That which it represents.

This sound when repeated acts as invocation to the deity. Yantra is the linear symbol of the same. Mantra is selected by Guru for the Sadhaka in consideration of disciple's latent capacity, constitution, temperament, maturity and advancement. Worship permissible to 'Vira' is denied to 'Pasu'. Each deity has its Mantra and Form for meditation. Suitability of particular Mantra is also judged from the first word in the name of the chanter and the first word of the Mantra and whether Mantra Tattva agrees with the Tattva of the chanter. Of all the yantras the Sri Chakra is very famous and is considered the eternal abode of Sri Lalita, the Supreme Deity in Samaya Marg:

Mahanirvana Tantra gives:

> *"Om Sat-Cid-Ekam Brahma"*
> *(Om-the one Being-Consciousness-Brahma)*
> *for meditation on Brahman.*

There is also *Brahma Gayatri* which reads:

> *"Parameshvaraya vidmahe*
> *Paratattvaya dhimahi*
> *Tanno brahma prachodayat"*

"May that Brahman whom we know and meditate upon to attain the Supreme Lord, the Supreme Reality, may He guide us."

Some Mantras are used in Shakti Sadhana e.g. *Hrim srim Krim Pa-ra-me-sva-ri-sva-ha.*

There are Bija Mantras for awakening Kundalini. Mantra and Tantra for each Chakra is separately laid down. The stress on certain syllables like *"Aim, Klim, Sauh"* on mantra, on diagram, on pronouncing the letters of Sanskrit alphabet in a certain way or their presence on petals of the Lotus, to be visualised on the Chakra, is in accordance with the ideals and usages of the time.*

Bija mantras are basic thought forms, living conscious sound powers. Meanings of some of the much used *bija mantras* are briefly given below:

---

* Those interested in further studies are referred to the following books:

1. *Principles of Tantra* by Sir J. Woodroffe.
2. *Serpent Power* by Sir J. Woodroffe.
3. *Mahanirvana Tantra* published by Ganesh and Co., Madras.
4. *Varivasys Rahasya* by Sri Bhaskararaya Makhin, Adyar Library & Research Centre.
5. *Sri Lalita Sahasra Namam* by Dr. C. Surya Narayanamurthy (Ganesh & Co.).
6. *Vijnana Bhairava Tantra* by Jaidev Singh.
7. *Mantra-Yantra-Tantra* by Devaraja Vidya Vachaspati.

AIM sound is bija mantra of the goddess of knowledge, Sarasvati, and is used for acquiring wisdom and command over language and speech.

HRIM sound represents Maya, the power of illusion, and is utilised for appeasing the Unmanifest and the power of Nature.

SRIM sound means limitlessness. It is bija mantra of Goddess Lakshmi, divinity of Fortune and Fate. It is recited in a prescribed manner for gaining wealth.

KLIM sound represents Form of Joy, Maheshvari, the power of Siva in the form of His consort, repeated for gaining pleasure, success, worldly power.

KRIM sound stands for the power of time, the power of death, the Goddess Kali, and is repeated for gaining transcendent knowledge and removing sorrow.

Lord Siva in loving dialogue with His consort, Parvati, mentioned in *Vijnana Bhairava Tantra,* a very ancient scripture reported to be 5000 years old, 112 methods of meditation. Some important techniques taken from it are given under respective yoga systems contained in this book. Some easy dharnas relating to Tantra are given below :

When a yogi contemplates with rapt attention on the whole universe and on his body as filled with eternal bliss, he will actually feel immersed in Divine Bliss.

Verse 65, *Vijnana Bhairava Tantra*

In coition, a person feels pleasure due to excitement. Delight in orgasm ensues from feeling of oneness and comes from one's own self, not from outside, as even without actual sexual union, there is delight in its memory. There is delight at the sight of a friend meeting after a long interval, or delight in eating and drinking. At the time of such intense pleasure, one should trace the source of pleasure and be absorbed in it.

Verses 69, 70, 71, *ibid*

A yogi may sit comfortably on a cushion, fully relaxed, and place one of his buttocks on the seat and keep his feet and arms free from any support. This posture will dispense with his mental tension and agitation.

Verse 78, *ibid*

By practising breath control, with sound and steadily contemplating in dvadasanta (12 fingers away from nostrils and 12 fingers inside) and in the heart centre at the time of sleep, he will have control over the dreams and death.

Verse 55, *Vijnana Bhairava Tantra*

In conclusion, it may be union of Kula Kundalini with Paramashiva in Sahasrara Chakra, or the state of choiceless awareness or a state of no mind, or union of the moon and sun (Ida and Pingala), of Prana and Apana, or Nada and Bindu or intense devotion and love for the beloved deity (Ishtadevata), or the selfless service of humanity, the meaning and ultimate aim in each case being the same. So follow any with earnestness, faith, perfect devotion and you are sure to achieve the goal.

All the important paths (yoga sadhanas) have been discussed in the foregoing chapters in a concise way. There may be some variations in other religions but there is hardly any difference in the basic principles and approach.

YANTRA or magical diagrams are geometrical figures, used in Tantra worship, made from linear elements intended to represent in a synthetic form, the principal powers of the natural world, which are Deities. They are the visual equivalents of the mantra or thought-forms. Yantra has mantra as its soul. Yantra is three-dimensional figure and should be conceived as solid. Yantras are symbolic representations as described below:

Bindu (Point) — All things and shapes are created from a point which develops into line, letter, word and sentence. It expresses the origin of manifestation, and nature of akasha (ether). When a point moves a line is formed. Point is Layasthana (point of merging).

A point placed in a circle shows umbilicus of manifestation.

A straight line shows straight movement and progress.

Circle — Circle is symbol of all cycles, rhythms, revolving movement (rajas tattva). It represents coalescence, esoterically 'the Egg of Brahma' *(Brahmanda)*, indicates union of consciousness and unconsciousness.

Triangle — An upward triangle represents fire and male principle. It is symbol of Siva, the Cosmic Being (Purusha).

Geometrical Figures—Magic Diagrams
(Constituent elements of Yantras)

Bindu (Point)

Line

Point in Circle

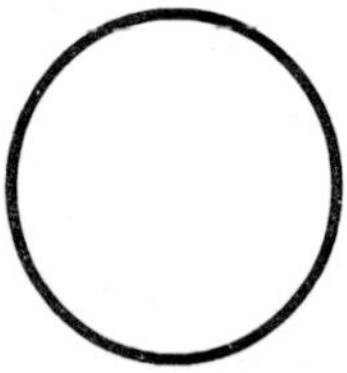

Circle

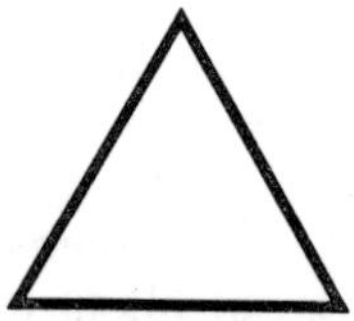

Triangle

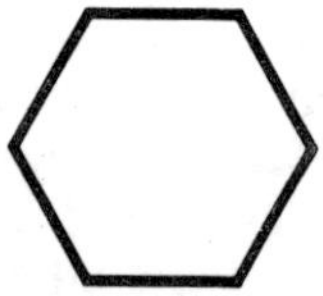

Hexagon

Square

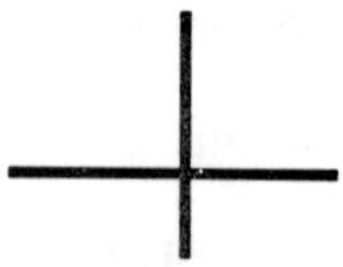

Cross

Cross

Cross in a Circle

Lotus

Trident

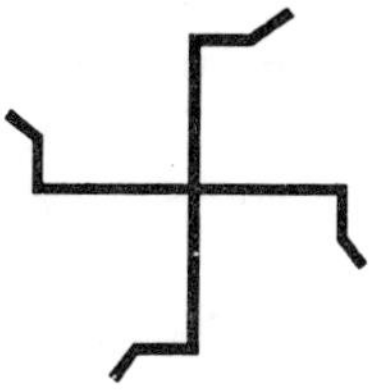

Svastika (Positive)

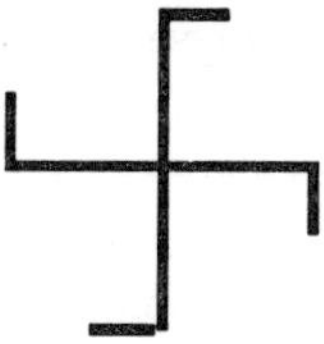

Svastika (Positive)

Svastika (Negative)

Pentagon

Hexagon

Hour-glass Siva's Drum

A triangle with its apex downward represents female organ, the emblem of energy (shakti) or Cosmic Nature (prakriti).

Triangle represents equilibrium of the basic forces, Trinity (Brahma, Vishnu, Rudra). It is also a sign for three gunas (*sattva, rajas, tamas*) and three humours (*vata, pitta* and *kapha*), which when in equilibrium in the body keep the person healthy. These are like positive, negative and earth wires of electricity.

Hexagon — shows vayu tattva (element of air).

Square — indicates earth and many-sidedness.

Cross — is symbol of expansion of a point in space and reduction of space to unity. It shows point expanding in all four directions and four perceptible elements.

Four-armed cross is symbol of Lord of Yajna. There is mystic cross, Egyptian cross, the Chinese Tau, cross of Rosicrucians, a cross of Christianity. A cross within a circle is churning of ocean of light space. (ksheera sagarmanthan).

Lotus — is symbol of chakra in the Kundalini.

Trident — (Trishoola) shows forces of dissolution, the three doshas, the forces of destruction. It also represents ichha (will), knowledge (jnana) and activity (kriya). It is a sign used by Paracelsus to overcome impotence.

Svastika — is used as an auspicious sign. It looks like letter Ga (ग) written on all four sides. It shows that supreme is beyond reach of human reason and intellect. It is a sign of victory and success. It is indicator of Lord Vishnu. Its four lines represent four arms of Lord Vishnu. Its centre is His *nabhi kamala* (navel point). Svastika with four dots and two associating lines represents Lord Ganapati. It is very ancient sign used by several nations and is also called Wheel of Law.

Star (Pentagon) — Many flowers have five petals. Reptiles, mammals and birds are generally five-toed. Man has five fingers, five sensory faculties (Jnana-indriyas) and five organs of action (karma-indriyas). There are five states of creative matter: earth, water, fire, air and ether. Number 5 is also associated with Lord Siva, the progenitor. This symbol shows love, passion and disintegration. It is also characteristic of Christian era. USSR, Muslim and United States use this as their emblem.

Star (Hexagon) —There are two triangles, one upright representing Purusha and the other downward indicating Prakriti. When they separate, the world ceases to exist.

The above-mentioned geometrical forms are expressions of cosmic forces or radiation and are combined for compilation of Yantras, which are then used, with appropriate mantras, for propitiation and invocation of certain cosmic forces.

Some yantras and charms are given on the next pages as examples for information and for creating further interest among the readers.

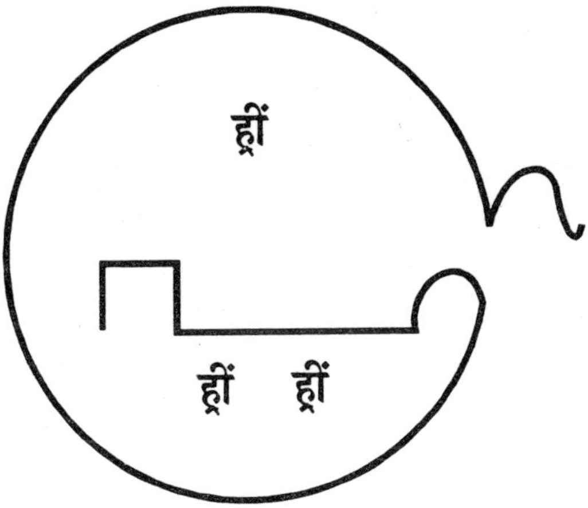

Yantra relating to Shloka 21 of *Saundarya-Lahari*

Sri Yantram relating to Shloka 22 of *Saundarya-Lahari*

Inscribed version of Sri Chakra (Wheel of Fortune) with some Sanskrit text.

I quote below two shlokas from *Saundarya Lahari* of Sri Samkara Bhagavat Pada, with their meaning and use.

Shloka 21

तडिल्लेखातन्वीं तपनशशिवैश्वानरमयीं
निषण्णां षण्णामप्युपरि कमलानां तव कलाम्
महापद्माटव्यां मृदितमलमायेन मनसा
महान्तः पश्यन्तोदधति परमानन्दलहरीम् ॥

Translation : Great men, who with their minds bereft of impurity and illusion, look on Thy Kala, slender as a streak of lightning, of the essence of Sun, Moon and Fire, and abiding in the great forest of lotuses, standing far above even the six lotuses, derive a flood of Infinite Bliss.

Yantra with Bija to be inscribed on Gold , Silver or Copper-plate. One thousand daily repetitions of this Mantras for 45 days for winning over the enemy are required. Food offering will include fruit, honey and jaggery.

Shloka 22

भवानि त्वं दासे मयि वितर दृष्टिं सकरुणा-
मिति स्तोतुं वाञ्छन्कथयति भवानि त्वमिति यः।
तदैव त्वं तस्मै दिशसि निजसायुज्यपदवीं
मुकुन्दब्रह्मेन्द्रस्फुटमुकुटनीराजितपदाम् ॥

Translation : When one, desirous of earnestly beseeching Thee with the words "O, Bhavani ! mayest thou cast Thy merciful glance on me, Thy slave" pronounces the words "Bhavani tvam" (May I be Thou) that very moment, Thou bestowest on him the status identically Thine Own, rendered lustrous by the brilliant crowns worn by Mukunda, Brahma and Indra.

Yantra with Bija mantra to be inscribed on Gold plate (to be worn as Talisman), Mantra to be repeated for 45 days at 1000 per day. Food offering: honey, trimadhura, curd, milk and spiced rice of various kinds. For attainment of all worldly desires and living above want.

KING OF YANTRA to gain all wordly desires and supernatural powers

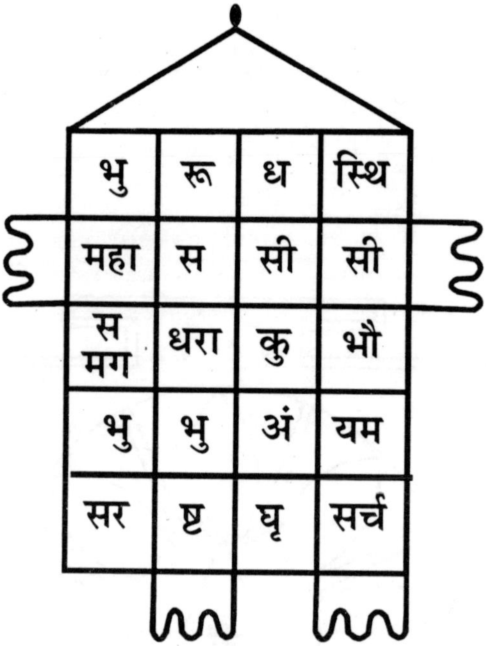

Yantra for protection from evil eye

र	र	र	र	र
र	र	र	र	र
र	र	र	र	र
र	र	र	र	र
र	र	र	र	र

Charm for return of wife to her husband, when charm is burried in the ash pit of her house

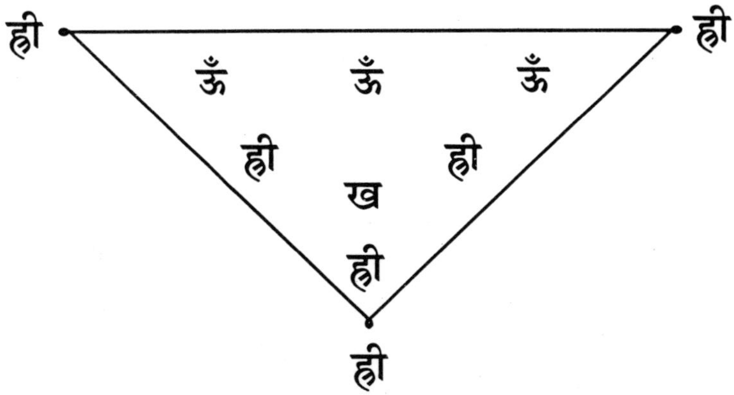

A charm to cure headache (worn on the body)

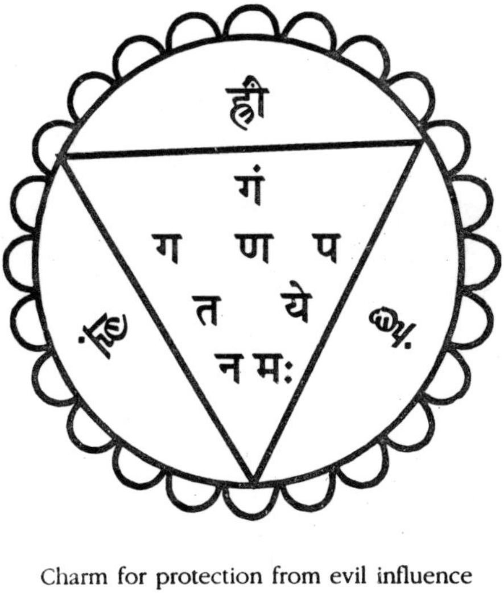

Charm for protection from evil influence

24

PREKSHA DHYANA

Literally 'Preksha Dhyana' means to witness, to see, to observe, to be vigilant, to see the mind with the mind, to feel the subtle vibrations in the body. This system, which consists of some techniques, already mentioned in this book at appropriate places, was discussed by me with Acharya Tulsi and Yuvacharya Shri Mahaprajna, the famous Jain saints, and is briefly mentioned below:

1. **Kayutsarg:** It consists of two main practices, firstly to relax physically and mentally in shavasana and secondly to shed egoism and self-pride, preceded by physical exercises, proper diet and good moral conduct. (See chapter on Ashtanga Yoga.)
2. **Bhava Kriya:** It is to be conscious of everything you do during the day while awake and also to live in the present, to work in the present and to think of the present, forget ting the past and not worrying for the future.
3. **Dirgha Svasha Preksha (Perception of Deep Breathing):** In breathing, upward and downward movements of the diaphragm cause contraction and relaxation of abdominal muscles and bioenergy is generated. Breathing should be deep, slow continuous and rhythmic. Perceive it by concentration inside the nostrils and observe closely where the breath touches the nostrils and the depth upto which it goes. (See Anapansati Yoga.)
4. **Samavritti Svasha Preksha (Perception of Breathing through Alternate Nostrils):** This is nadi-shodhana (purifying of subtle nerves). Inhale from the left nostril by closing the right nostril by thumb and exhale from the right by closing the left with index finger. Reverse the position and do it alternately. Inhaling time should be less than the exhaling time (ratio 1:2). Concentrate your mind on inhaling and exhaling. Mind can be

controlled by watching the breathing process. When mind is calm, breathing is slow and placid and so when breathing is slow, smooth and less, mind becomes peaceful. Rate of breathing per minute can be reduced from normal 15-17 to 4-5 to achieve tranquillity. (See Paranayama in Patanjali's Ashtang Yoga.)

5. **Sharira Preksha (Perception of Body):** Our body is a great workshop in which various complicated, chemical, mechanical and electromagnetic processes are constantly going on. In this method mind's eye is gently focussed on the internal complex of activities, to revitalize them with our will power starting from the top of the head and going slowly to the toes of the feet and concentrating at each organ, mind, eyes, ears, mouth, neck, heart, lungs, liver, pancreas, kidneys and so on. Remain conscious of the vibrations of the vital dormant energy in the body, filling and energising each organ, each cell, inside and outside.
6. **Chaitanya Kendra Preksha (Perception of Psychic Centres):** Modern medical science has found that neuro-endocrine system exerts great influence on emotions, mental states, and behavioural patterns of a person. Wilful concentration on various endocrine glands in human body can change/improve the secretations of harmones, para-harmones, and neuroharmones, which can alter the blood chemistry and can ennoble the character and habits of a person. Concentrate on each Chakra, starting from Muladhara Chakra (plexus) and witness the subtle vibrations in each centre, going up to Sahasrara chakra. (See chapter on Kundalini Yoga.)
7. **Laisha Dhyana (Perception of Colours):** Acharya Tulsi has given different names for the traditional names of the centres (chakras) viz. Shanti Kendra, Drishti Kendra, Joti Kendra, Gyan Kendra etc.) Colours to be visualised are in relations to human aura (astral body, see Chapter 3 Good Health). Visualise green colour disk (Halo) at Anahata chakra (Shanti Kendra) blue colour at Vishudha chakra, red at Ajna chakra, yellow, Golden disk in the forehead and white shining disk in the Sahasrara chakra.

These techniques increase mental power, memory, reduce tension and cure several diseases.

PART II

INVOCATIONS AND MISCELLANEOUS

25

UNTO BLISS

The eternal and abiding peace for which you hunt outside in vain, is within you—in the deep recesses of your heart, ever-ready and anxious to embrace you and to fill you with its divine sweetness, supreme calmness and profound love. You say that the world is full of worries, miseries; but your Mind creates the world you complain of! Why not change your Mind and so your world too?

Like a cocoon, you are always weaving threads of thoughts which keep you imprisoned, involved or enveloped, never allowing a restful moment; only sleep gives it a little pause.

Retire to a place of perfect solitude, sit erect in a comfortable posture, breathe slowly and softly, stop the wheel of bubbling thoughts and be calm, tranquil and serene, as much as you can, like the unwavering flame of candle. Relax every nerve and cell of your body and forget it. Drive off politely all thoughts, desires, fancies and forget them. Clear your conscience and empty your mind, creating a sort of blankness. Be in perfect silence and watch choicelessly.

Nature abhors a vacuum. Lo! you are filled with perfect Peace and Happiness. You are nearing your Real Self, discovering your potentialities, and unity with the *WHOLE* which is timeless, spaceless and limitless.

Why do you confine yourself and limit your possibilities and energies which are vast and infinite? Why not submit and surrender to Him and His will which is none else but your own and is true by rooting out the little 'self' and making room for the play of Divine Life, Light, Love and Truth.

Peace be unto you!

26

DEVOTEE'S PRAYER

My Lord, All-gracious, All-powerful, All-knowing and All-doing Father, I bow to Thee with heartiest and sincerest love and humbleness. Thou art the Beginningless Beginning of the whole Cosmos. Thou art the Eternal Time. Thou art the Ancient One, the Immense Being. Thou art the life and light of the Universe and moveth and ruleth it in the most wonderful and surprising manner, that a humble and frail being like man can never know with his limited powers, which too are blessed by Thee. I rejoice within to remember Thee. I wonder at the vast sky, myraid of stars, moons and suns, 100 billion galaxies each having more than 100 billion stars, studded unimaginably in the space like precious gems in a dark-blue velvet. The great black hole consuming stars into itself and a Halo of Gas extending 1200 light years across the space, with temperature of 3.5 million fahrenheit, capable of creating 10000 suns, are wonders of wonders!

On the earth I live, I see boundless seas with strange creatures, the bottom of the sea with marvellous beauty of its own, the thick forests fraught with innumerable kinds of animals, the vast plains, the lovely hills and valleys, the highest snow-capped peaks of the Everest in the dead silence of the ranges of Himalayas, all full of excellent natural scenery, art and beauty. How various kinds of flower grow from the same earth and contain a variety of colours and fragrances, and even a butterfly, a fish has thousand of varieties of colours and designs.

Here, I see definite, intelligent laws responsible for harmonious existence of the universe for countless ages. There is eternal law, order, system and method in everything, from the tiniest atom to the supergalactic universes. All this is puzzling to the human mind, Thy superior creation. It is impossible to describe even the minutest part of a dust particle, that Thou hast made.

Master of infinite resources! All-knowing Intelligence, Thou hast sent me in Thy world. Why? Thou better knoweth, I prostrate myself before Thee and most humbly seek to be guided along the Right Path. Let me be Thine, filled with the purest and sublimest love! My most Benevolent Lord, give me strength enough to fulfil my duties, to abide by Thy Laws and Commands and to lead a happy fruitful life!

Finally, if I live, I should live to use my passions and sentiments righteously, to realise myself, to feel and breathe with every human being and to worship Thee, My most kind Father, Let me be Thine and let Thou be mine. Pray accept this humble prayer of mine, O God Divine!

Give me O, Lord, the eye that
seeth and with the craze of
love, do Thou fill my head!

Jalaluddin Rumi

27

MOTHER DIVINE

Thou art the creator and sustainer of the Universe in all its forms. Thou keepeth the planets in their proper orbits. Thou shineth in the sun, the moon, the stars and the Milky path of the sky. Thou art the vast unimaginable space which fills the skies. Thou art the Life and Light. Thou art the Energy—Electricity which permeates the whole creation from an atom to the Milky Way. Thou thunderth in the clash of the clouds. Thou moveth in the air, floweth in the water, shineth forth in the light, heateth the fire. Thou art the sweetness of the song, the melody of the music, the beauty of the beautiful, the fragrance of the flowers, the glory of Nature, the colours of the rainbow, the ecstasy of the ascetic. Thou permeateth and pervadeth the Universe.

Hail, Hail to Thee, Divine Mother, a thousand times all Hail!

I prostrate before Thee. I do homage to Thee, I am in Thy loving care. Thou art full of love, mercy and grace. Thou art the embodiment of Eternal Bliss. Thou art the expression, manifestation of the Unseen and Unknowable, the changing phenomena of the Unchangeable, the visible variety of the Invisible One, the qualities of the Unqualified and Impersonal, the cause of the Causeless!

My profound salutations and adorations to Thee, Mother Divine!

How can I, a frail human being, define Thee, who art beyond description, imagination and thought, who cannot be conceived through the mind, intellect or understanding? Thy reign begins where the kingdom of thought ends, where the flight of intellect lies exhausted in despair, and where Science is mum and dumb! Thou giveth a clue to the Unknowable; but inseparable from That, like the negative and positive poles of the magnet, like the pleasure and pain of the mundane life.

Thou art supreme, sublime and all-merciful! Hail! Hail! to Thee!

The mother on earth is Thy humble shadow of Divine mercy. When an earthly mother does so much for her child, how could Thou be caring for me! Dear and revered Mother, I approach Thee with folded palms, with tears in my eyes, with heart surging with emotions of love and devotion, with mind clinging at Thy Lotus-Feet—what else can I bring to Thee—what offerings can I make—all is Thine, these too are Thine. Pray take me in Thy lap, protect me, guide me, lead me through the Path of Light to the Lighthouse of Thy Grace, from the darkness of illusion and ignorance towards the sunshine of Knowledge, Bliss, where there is Eternal Peace and no return!

Hail! Hail! to Thee Mother, million times all Hail!
Each pore and cell of my body sings Thy Glory!

I humbly beseech Thee to awaken the dormant serpent power (Kundalini Shakti) latent in me, to raise the current higher, and higher, to fill me with absolute peace and perfection to merge my little 'self' into the Overself, to break my limitations in the cosmic store-house of Infinite Energy. Thou art the only Guide to lead me on in the difficult path towards the destination!

O Mother of Joy, O Mother of love, O Mother of beauty, O Mother of Kundalini, O Mother Supreme, pray lead me on!

My profound salutation and adorations to Thee, Divine Mother!

28

AUTO-SUGGESTION FOR HEALTH

O Indweller of my Heart! Thou permeateth every cell of my body and causeth the cells to move and work. It is with Thy power that my body carries out all functions and lives. The moment Thou goeth out of this physical frame, it lies dead and lifeless!

While I sleep, Thou art awake and carrieth out the beating of the heart, the pumping of the blood, the digesting of the food and the repairing of the fatigued limbs. Thou art the source of Life and Energy! Fill my body with health and vitality! Let my organs function properly! Let my digestion be strong, my blood pure and my eyes lustrous!

Thou art the store of Infinite Knowledge and Bliss! Let all healthy and positive thoughts come to my brain from all sides. Let good thoughts go from my brain in all directions and help others! Let my mind be filled with thoughts of love, faith and sympathy for all! Let my mind be calm and serene! Let it be peaceful and happy! Let it rejoice within and taste the nectar divine!

Thou art the Supreme Healer, the greatest of all physicians and surgeons! Pray save me from disease! Free me from weaknesses of all kinds! Thy name is the greatest Tonic! May the nectar flowing from the repetition of Thy name rejuvenate my system and soothe and strengthen my nerves!

Let me inhale energy from surrounding atmosphere which is saturated with Thy subtle cosmic power! Let my lungs suck the vitality from the air inhaled and let them exhale the carbon-dioxide of negative thoughts and germs of ill and ailments! Let them throw out in each exhalation all undesirable elements from my system.

Thou art the secret of Health and Happiness! While I pray, my body and mind are at perfect rest and ease! Each and every cell of my body is being relaxed and renewed! These cells are keeping me young and healthy. These are filled with capacity to work without fatigue and depression! My sexual energy is being sublimated into divine lustre *(Ojas and Tejas)*! I am getting strong, healthy and young day by day and turning this physical body into a fit receptacle of divine Light and Life.

29

THE DIVINE PLAY

Why do you lose the joy of life considering yourself as a 'doer' and creating the false sense of 'I' and 'mine'? Why not become the onlooker and watch this Eternal Dance of Seen and Unseen ever going on in the Universe?

If you entertain the idea as an actor or doer, you cannot enjoy the show and are caught in the whirlpool of actions. So why not remain aloof from inside, while moving and acting with Divine Will and derive fullest joy of existence ? Witness silently this wonderful Drama of Life, full of Divine Glory and Grandeur. You can only appreciate its beauty, if you look on it as a spectator without reaction, without revaluation, without attachment and choice.

Before a child is born, Nature provides milk in the mother's breast. So worrying for that which need not be worried about or grieving for that which should not be grieved for, why do you unnecessarily burden yourself with care and responsibility which are not yours? Why not mind your own work and leave the rest to God Who is the Primal Cause of Whole creation!

30

PRAYER FOR THE CONTROL OF MIND

O Indweller of my Heart, I surrender my humble self to Thy care! Take me under Thy shelter, attract me as a magnet attracts iron filings, as the moon attracts the waves and causes periodical tides in the ocean, as a lotus allures a *Bhramar* and flowers fascinate nightingales and butterflies by their sweet fragrance, as the earth attracts all objects towards its centre and the moon makes a *chakor* to fly towards it; similarly draw my restless mind, which is deep like a sea and powerful like an elephant, towards Thee by Thy Divine Grace!

Alone, I am weak and helpless, my existence is no existence, but with Thy Effulgence and Grace, I become powerful and able to guide the stumbling mind to the righteous path. I shall be careful of its clever moves and persuasions. Oh, this mind is very tricky and unsteady, the perishable youth and beauty, the temporary pleasures of the world tempt it and then betray it! It becomes unsteady and uncontrollable and I become helpless at its hands. I feel and realise my weakness. But my Lord! Thou could give me strength and perseverance! If Thou can control and guide the infinite Universe of unconceivable greatness, with its starry heavens, how trifling it is for you to help me in control of my mind!

If, once for a moment, I get a glimpse of Thy Divine Form, or taste the Divine Nectar of ecstasy, mundane pleasures will look shallow and tasteless and my mind will not go towards them off and on; just as a person who after having tasted a sweet mango will not go after or like a sour one.

Pray, do not discard me and move me away from Thy Lotus-feet! I have taken refuge under Thy care being disappointed and driven away from all directions! If Thou dost not protect me, what would the world say? Thou art the Supreme Protector! Thou art my everything! This body is Thy temple. Thou seest from my eyes, hearest from my ears, moveth and worketh from this body! Thou art the temple, the devotee and the Lord, all together, the Trinity!

As impure water becomes pure by merging in the river Ganga, as a drop of water becomes a part and parcel of the ocean by uniting with the ocean and losing its identity and limitations, just as water adopts the shape of milk when mixed with milk, so do I change into Supreme Soul by breaking through my casket of ignorance and realising my Eternal Unity with Thee!

As a river is earnest to join the ocean, and travels hard and long for this union, as a fish becomes restless and desperate to go into the water from the moment it is taken out, as a faithful and devoted woman pines for the return of her beloved husband, and as a hungry person becomes lifeless without food, so do I crave Thy Divine Embrace, and union with Thee for ever and anon!

Be pleased to accept me as Thy humble devotee. How lucky is the dust particle that clingest to Thy lotus feet!

For the sake of spirit, O mind!
Let go all these wandering thoughts.

Rigveda IX.112.3

31

INVOKING THE DIVINE GRACE

O Indweller of my heart! Thou maketh this body move and work. It is by Thy power that my heart beats, the blood runs in the arteries, the breath comes in and goes out. My eyes see, ears hear, nose smells, brain thinks, heart loves and hates, I strive and struggle; but how is it that Thou always remaineth hidden from me?

While hidden in the innermost recesses of my heart, Thou ever guideth and directeth all the functions of my body and mind. While the body develops, it also wanes, ages and deteriorates. Thy presence is ever felt with the same perpetual intensity, that never undergoes a change. That is eternal and constant.

Thou art the Source of Intelligence and Knowledge. Thou art the sailor of this life-boat across the ocean of the world (Samsara). Then why dost Thou accuseth me for the deeds done under the impulse and with the vitality and life bestowed by Thee, while I cannot stir or think without the light and life borrowed from Thee.

Thou art the source of all sources, the support of all supports and cause of all causes. Thou art the vitality and life that keepth the cells of the body to maintain their form and shape. Thou art the Existence. Now that I have traced Thee behind these gross sheaths, names and forms, pray, come out of Thy hiding place and reveal Thyself to me!

If Thou thinketh this physical body unfit for Thy expression, or manifestation, then make it fit! Thou art the maker, the builder, the life-giver, controller, and the be-all and end-all of all Existence.

I am nothing without Thee. Even 'nothingness' cannot be without Thee. Pray, reveal Thyself and fill me with true love and devotion for Thee. Take me to the innermost chamber of Thy retreat, where Thou withdraweth from outward manifestation and let me share Thy Divine Bliss. Pray, light the in and out of this humble self with Thy Effulgent bountiful Grace!

May Divine peace reign in my heart!

O Thou self-revealing One
Reveal Thyself to me,
Thou who art the spirit of manifestation,
Manifest Thyself to me.

32

OFFERINGS

O Lord of the Universe, Thou art the mysterious indefinable latent Power that pervadeth everything and governeth and ruleth the Seen and Unseen worlds with perfect law and order. Thou art the Intelligence and Life working behind the natural phenomena. Regularity and definite principles of working found in every act and atom of Nature remind us of Thy stupendous Power.

The millions of moons and stars, the countless worlds that look like tiny little twinkling, lightspots, on the dark night overhead, whose light travelled for millions of years to reach our eyes, the fathomless oceans, the gigantic rivers, the huge forests and beasts and countless species of creatures that inhabited and now inhabit the earth, sea and air, the snow-peaked mountains, the huge glaciers, the highest peak of Everest, the sandy deserts with their formidable sand storms, the snowy poles of the earth and all from the tiny blade of grass to the Nebula of stars, speak of Thy indefinable glory and splendour. This humble self sings Thy praise from every pore and cell of this body. The tears of ecstasy roll down my cheeks and I stand in awe and reverence, meek and humble at Thy open door!

The Light in my heart beckons me to seek within to approach Thee at the shrine of my heart, where Thou carrieth all functions silently and smoothly and moveth this miniature body in the most extraordinary and mysterious way.

The variety in the Universe surprises and overwhelms me. The more I know, the more I seek, the more I find myself ignorant and far from the vast fathomless Ocean of Knowledge which knows no bounds. The complete knowledge of an atom has not come even after thousands of years of research. The span of life is too short and art too long! I am puzzled! What is That by knowing which everything is known ? Who is that seeking whom everything comes by itself ? What is that by holding which one catches the Infinity ? An Inner Voice whispers faintly That is none else but Thee and Thee alone!

My Lord, I have come to Thee empty-handed without rituals, formalities and preparations. I know no *Yoga* or *Japa*, science of worship or methods of approach and prayer. I have nothing else except this little 'self' and flowers of love and devotion. Pray, accept these humble offerings, dedicated with all sincerity of heart at Thy Lotus-Feet and bless this humble worshipper with Thy Grace!

33

THE SECRET OF HAPPINESS

It is the forgetfulness of the little 'self' or 'I', which fills man with happiness or gives pleasures, depending in each case upon the duration and nature of the forgetfulness. For example, when he likes a delicious dish, for the time being he loses himself in the relish of the food and momentarily the 'I' vanishes from his consciousness, giving him the feeling of satisfaction or pleasure. Similarly, a lover forgets himself in the fascinating beauty of his beloved; in her gleaming eyes, he sees the brightness of the moon, in her lips he finds the odour and smell of roses, and in her smile, the coolness of breeze. His attachment and love overflows and he forgets everything, even his own self. He could not understand that it is he who makes her so. Writers, scholars, philosophers, scientists, inventors and founders, all forget themselves when absorbed in their work. Their interest in the undertaking deepens the concentration; the work becomes the main object of their lives, and in that they merge and lose themselves. To lose oneself is to find oneself. But to forget the self by merging in worldly objects which change, is a momentary and temporary satisfaction or pleasure. To achieve permanent and eternal peace, therefore, one has to associate oneself with an unchanging Entity, so that when he is absorbed in That there is no break or return but an eternal forgetfulness and annihilation of the 'I'. The streamlet of little 'I' merges in the vast ocean of universal Spirit ending its limitations and partaking of the powers and resources of the vast and fathomless sea.

34

INDRIYAS — THE BEST SERVANTS

Why do you fear the sense-organs? Why do you blame them? These are the instruments of gaining knowledge and are not to be hated and despised. These are useful limbs created by Nature for looking at this wonderful universe, a work of art and beauty. Look at the colourful flowers, green bushes, tall trees, humming bees, smiling buds and running brooks! You cannot count their varieties. They are so many. Look at the blue sky, the star-studded dark night and shining full moon instilling nectar in herbs and fruits, for you to enjoy their taste and delicacy.

The supremacy of human intelligence, the beauty of the female figure, the fragrance of the roses and lilies, the thrill and soft kiss of the morning breeze, the dew drops on lotus leaves, flying of birds in flocks! You could not have enjoyed all the Divine Play (Lila) if your senses were not there.

When senses are extrovert, you enjoy the Divine Play, the Eternal Dance (the world and its beauty). When you take the senses inward to look inside and make them introvert, you can enjoy the latent panorama of Divine Play inside. By closing your ears, you will begin to hear the melodious Anahata sounds, which are peculiar, sweet and melodious, unlike any worldly music. If you shut your eyes, and concentrate between the two eyebrows, you will see the Effulgent Lights shining but cool, pleasant and unparalleled. If you direct your mind to the inward path, it will lead you to the gate of Silence.

Though eyes cannot see Him, yet it is due to Him that eyes see. Though ears cannot hear Him, yet it is due to Him, that ears hear. Though mind cannot think of Him, yet it is on His account that mind thinks.

He is beyond the senses, yet reveals Himself through the senses to the chosen few.

Therefore, all the senses have purpose and use. They have to be utilised properly and wisely.

Be their Master and use them for right purpose, in right manner, at right time and enjoy life to the fullest.

If you find fault with chariot (body) or horses (senses) no good purpose will be served. You have to learn to use them, to control them with awareness and attention.

> 'May my senses always live in harmony and create harmony for others'.
>
> *Taittiriya Upanishad*

> *Divinity dwells in speech as the power to protect, in the in-breath and the out-breath as power to take and give,*
> *in the hands as the power to act,*
> *in the feet as the power to move,*
> *in the anus as the power of riddance.*
> *In the world of elements, it dwells in rain as the power to quench,*
> *In thunder as strength, in cattle as wealth.*
> *It dwells as light in the stars,*
> *in sperm as the power of generation, and in sex as pleasure.*
> *It dwells in ether as (the support of) all.*
> *And where it dwells, there it must be worshipped.*
>
> *Taittiriya Upanishad*, III.10

BIBLIOGRAPHY

Autobiography of a Yogi by Paramahansa Yogananda

Bhagavad Gita translated by Dr. S. Radhakrishnan

Bhagavad Gita, Gita Press, Gorakhpur

Book of Secrets by Acharya Sri Rajneesh

Chakras by C.W. Leadbeater

Devatma Shakti (Kundalini) by Swami Vishnu Tiratha

Discovery of India by Jawahar Lal Nehru

Dhyana Chakra, Gurudev Ashram, Ganeshpuri

Essays on Gita by Sri Aurobindo

Encyclopaedia of World Religions, Octopus Book Ltd

Freedom from Known by J. Krishnamurti

Gandhiji: His Life and Work, published on his 75th birthday

Gitanjali by Rabindra Nath Tagore

Gita Explained by Dhyaneshwar Maharaj, Translation by Manu Subedar

Gita Pravachan by Acharya Vinoba

How to be a Yogi by Swami Abhedanand

Hinduism in Space Age by E. Vedavyas

Hindu Polytheism by Alain Danielou (Routledge and Kegan Paul, London)

Hymns from Rigveda by Jean Le Mee

Hatha Yoga by Swami Sivananda

Introduction to Tantra Shastra by Sir John Woodroffe

Inner Reality by Paul Brunton

In the Woods of God-Realization by Swami Ram Tirtha

Incredible India by P. Thomas

Incredible Sai Baba by Arthor Osborne

Indian History and Culture by J. Fuste & I.R. Mehta

Kalyana Kalpataru, January, *1940,* Gita Press, Gorakhpur

Karma Yoga by Swami Vivekananda

Law of Success by Napolean Hill

Layman's Guide to Psychiatry and Psychoanalysis by Eric Berne M.D.

Meditation, Sri Aurobindo Ashram

Mental Health in Theory and Practice by Bhadur Mal

Mind by Rene Dubos, Henry Margenau

Mind Mechanism (Vols.I to VIII) by Warren Milton

My Experiments with Truth by Mahatma Gandhi

Mysterious Kundalini by Vasant G. Rele

Mysticism (Vols. I & II) by L.R. Puri

Practice of Bhakti Yoga by Swami Sivananda

Psychology of Every Man and Woman by A.E. Mander

Raja Yoga by Swami Vivekanand

Religion and Modern Doubts by Swami Nirvedananda

Right Thinking by H.T. Hamblin

Science of Being and Art of Living by Maharshi Mahesh Yogi

Search in Secret India by Paul Brunton

Secret Path by Paul Brunton

Studies in Tantra and Vedas by M.P. Pandit

Sure Ways of Success in Life and God Realization by Swami Sivananda

Sadhana by Rabindra Nath Tagore

Sadhana by Swami Sivananda

Saundarya Lahari by Sri Samkara Bhagavat Pada

Serpent Power by Sir John Woodroffe

Swadhyaya Sudha, Shree Gurudev Asharam, Ganeshpuri

Ten Great Cosmic Powers by S. Shankaranarayanan

Ten Points to Health by Sri Balasaheb Pandit (Pratinidhi, Raja of Audh)

Think and Grow Rich by Napolean Hill.

Tradition and Revolution by J. Krishnamurti

Ultimate Alchemy (Vols. I and II) by Acharya Shree Rajneesh

Vijnana Bhairava Tantra by Jaidev Singh

What is Meditation by Acharya Rajneesh

Why Meditation by Vimala Thakar

Yoga by Dr. Phulgenda Sinha

Yoga Alpha and Omega (Vols. I and II) by Acharya Shri Rajneesh

Yoga and Health by Elisabeth Haich, translated by Selvarajan Yesudian.

INDEX

J

K

L

M

N

O

P

R

S

OTHER IMPORTANT NEW AGE BOOKS

THE YOGA OF LOVE (Based on Sri Aurobindo's Synthesis of Yoga) *—M.P. Pandit*

Love is the crown of knowledge. True knowledge ends in love, even as real, wide, spontaneous love which is either vouchsafed to one or springs from the fount of the heart leads one to the perception of the existence of God everywhere. Love opens many windows on the Reality that is God; one cannot escape perceiving God when one is filled with love for God. Even as knowledge culminates in love, love leads to an integral knowledge.

ISBN: 81-7822-057-1

THE YOGA OF SELF-PERFECTION (Based on Sri Aurobindo's Synthesis of Yoga)*—M.P. Pandit*

The Yoga of Self-Perfection recognizes a Divine purpose in life and starts from the premise that the ultimate aim of life is not simply escape, but rather, to work out the divine perfection in manifestation.

ISBN: 81-7822-077-6

THE YOGA OF WORKS (Based on Sri Aurobindo's Synthesis of Yoga) *—M.P. Pandit*

The Yoga of Works is perhaps the first and most important aspect of yoga for seekers to take up. It deals with the problems of—energy, action and direction which confronts us all whenever we try to integrate our spiritual aspirations with the daily life around us and the need to "work" in the society and play a role in the vast undertakings of the Western world.

ISBN: 81-7822-079-2

KUNDALINI YOGA (A Brief Study of Sir John Woodroff's "The Serpent Power")*—M.P. Pandit*

The search for inner awakening and unfolding of hidden powers has brought man to the threshold of the last frontier: himself. For it is deep within that we find the secret key and unlock the door long held secure from our sight. The ancient philosopher's call "Know Thyself" continues to beckon us on the path of knowledge as the final object of our ongoing investigation.

ISBN: 81-7822-076-8

THE BOOK OF CHAKRA HEALING*—Liz Simpson*

The Book of Chakra Healing is a comprehensive guide to the ancient Indian system of chakras. These centres of "spinning energy" in the body help to maintain your physical, mental, emotional, and spiritual balance. This book offers practical way to work on your chakras and shows you how to unblock and rebalance your energy. This book will be of great benefit to both health care professionals and lay people and will inspire many to explore and develop their relationship with an integral part of their being—the chakras.

ISBN: 81-7822-043-1

THE SELF-REVEALED KNOWLEDGE THAT LIBERATES THE SPIRIT
—*Roy Eugene Davis*

In this book the author presents a clear explanation of the soul's awakening through progressive stages of spiritual growth from ordinary, illusional states of awareness to mental illumination, spiritual enlightenment, and liberation of consciousness. The descriptions of philosophical principles will satisfy the rational mind and speak to the heart that aspires to direct perception of truth.

ISBN: 81-7822-050-4

THE HEALING HANDBOOK (A Spiritual Guide to Healing Yourself and Others)—*Tara Ward*

In this book the author presents a range of techniques and tools for healing yourself and other, including children and animals. The book features: Techniques for chakra awareness, relaxation, self-assessment, releasing anger and resentment, healing physical conditions, creating a healing sanctuary, increasing sensitivity, developing intuition, protecting yourself, absent healing and provides information about healing tools such as pendulums, crystals, colour, sound, massage, spirit guides.

ISBN: 81-7822-034-2

HEALING THE FUTURE (The Journey Within)—*Deepak Kashyap*

The greatest possibilities of body-cure, says the author, lie in forgetting the body. To the extent we lose body-consciousness and identify with the Spirit, physical disability and mental trauma disappearing on their own. *Healing the Future* is then, an attempted tip-off on the little secrets of holistic living that can be mastered in easy, small steps. This book urges you to treat consciousness as a canvas, and begin adding new colour, shine and texture to your tomorrow from this very instant.

ISBN: 81-7822-039-3

STRESS-FREE WORK WITH YOGA AND AYURVEDA
—*Vinod Verma*

Dr. Verma's advice for a stress-free work environment begins with a daily yoga program. The aim of this book is to provide a guide for building a better work atmosphere based on an understanding of Ayurvedic personality types—according to your fundamental nature or *prakriti*. It is also important to learn how to acquire a state of satisfaction in your personal life, which is essential for both better work performance and your health. It helps you to build your own good atmosphere—even in the worst of circumstances.

ISBN: 81-7822-000-8

CHAKRA ENERGY MASSAGE (Spiritual Evolution into the Subconscious Through Activation of the Energy Points of the Feet)—*Marianne Uhl*

This book guides you into the fascinating world of the energy body. Drawing on the knowledge gained by Foot Reflexology Massage, it introduces you to the Chakra Energy Massage. By means of the fine energy channels connecting them to the body's organs and energy centres, our feet reflect our physical and psychic condition. It enables you to acquire basic knowledge needed for Foot Reflexology Massage and Chakra Energy Massage.

ISBN: 81-7822-004-0